Use Your
Authenticity
Advantage

BECAUSE PRETENDING IS EXHAUSTING!

T J GILROY

Tremendous Leadership

PO Box 267

Boiling Springs, PA 17007

(717) 701 - 8159 • (800) 233 - 2665

www.TremendousLeadership.com

Use Your Authenticity Advantage: Because Pretending is Exhausting!.

ISBN-13 978-1-949033-70-0

DESIGNED & PRINTED IN THE UNITED STATES OF AMERICA

Contents

Chapter 1
What Do You Want?

The onus of discovering your Authenticity Advantage is on you.

Why do I say that? Many people have been led to believe that their company, their organization, or their government will help them to be all they can be. Well, have you noticed that whatever organization you belong to really doesn't care whether you are authentic or not? But you should. It's not their purpose to help you to be authentic, it's yours.

Organizations care about their missions much more than they care about individuals. Military commanders who put their people above completing their missions will soon find themselves removed from command. Company executives who value their people over profits will soon be looking for new careers. So, whose job is it for you to become your best self? You guessed it; the onus is on you.

If you are reading this book, you have probably already come to that conclusion. Also, you probably feel that you are not living as the person God created you to be. You are not your best self.

You probably don't know what you want, do you?

You probably don't really know who you are either, do you?

That's a problem! But you are not alone. These issues are widespread, and very few people know what to do about them.

If you don't know what you want to do or to have, or if what you think you want seems to be out of your grasp, then the reason is that you don't know who you are. Your lack of authenticity is keeping you from all you are supposed to have in this life.

You may be in a time of transition, searching for a fulfilling career, entering a new phase of life, looking for better relationships, or trying to figure out how you can make a difference. But how do you find these things?

I'm glad you asked.

You were born with all the attributes you need to be successful in a way that is specific to you. Those attributes are your Authenticity Advantage. Sadly, many trade their Authenticity Advantage for a lesser life to "fit in" with a world that expects them to do and have what others have deemed appropriate. Both the proliferation of social media and our innate desire for comparison help to drive many people's desires to conform. They fall into the trap of trying to imitate someone else's success rather than finding their own authentic way.

Imitating someone else will never give you the same great level of satisfaction and fulfillment as being who you were created to be. You may have heard this before, but it is true: you will make a poor somebody else, but a great you.

When you try to succeed in life by ignoring who you really are, everything becomes a struggle. It's exhausting!

In This Book You Will Learn

1. Who you really are.
2. What you want to do.
3. What you want to have.

You will discover that passion overcomes obstacles and struggles, exhaustion can be replaced by exhilaration, and your choices should be made from your purpose in life. When you realize how uniquely you think and just how special that is, you will understand why I call that your GIFT and why I capitalize it throughout the rest of this book.

You will naturally want to use your GIFT (the unique and special way you think as evidenced by a single talent that can be developed to greatness) to fulfill all your heart's desires. You will also discover that it is much more fun to go through life with purpose than on the roller coaster ride of ups and downs caused by drifting.

How Authenticity Advantage Is Different

If you search for books dealing with authenticity, you will find no less than 50 titles. If you search for blog posts or articles written about authenticity, you will find even more to read.

Until now, most of what has been written about authenticity may provide you with some thoughts on how to become more authentic, or it might tell you reasons why being authentic is important. It might also tell you how prevalent the problem of not being authentic is. You might even become acquainted with assessments to learn more about yourself. It seems each book, each blog post, and each assessment claim to have the answer.

However, your authentic self is much more complicated. No single approach can give you a complete perspective on who you really are. Let me explain.

After I left the military for the business world, I discovered the personal development industry. (Yes, there is an entire industry devoted to helping you grow personally and professionally, of which I was completely ignorant while in the Marines.) When I was introduced to personality assessments as part of my personal development plan, I thought I died and went to heaven. It explained so much of why I was struggling.

Then I learned about love languages. That explained even more about my marriage and relationships in general. But wait, there's more! Then I learned about strengths assessments and discovered even more about the real me and how I had been missing the mark.

Which one of the many assessments or perspectives do you follow or focus on? What happens when you realize some of them contradict each other? That's when confusion can set in.

For example, one of my favorite quotes from my personal development studies came from Calvin Coolidge who said:

> *Nothing in this world can take the place of persistence. Talent will not: nothing is more common than unsuccessful men with talent. Genius will not: unrewarded genius is almost a proverb. Education will not: the world is full of educated derelicts. Persistence and determination alone are omnipotent.*

Cool quote, right? It leads one to believe that hard work and persistence are the only things that matter. Dominant, directing, doer types of leaders with exceptional self-discipline love this quote.

But then I read an equally inspiring, but contradictory, quote from the famous business and management guru, Peter Drucker, who said:

> *Most people think they know what they are good at. They are usually wrong. More often, people know what they are not good at—and even then more people are wrong than right. And yet, a person can perform only from strength. One cannot build performance on weakness, let alone on something one cannot do at all.*

So, which is the real key to success: persistence that overcomes weaknesses without regard for talent or building strengths instead of overcoming weaknesses? Can you see the potential for confusion? This is why I want to help you put the pieces together so you can find your Authenticity Advantage.

There is no cookie cutter solution, but there are some very valuable tools that can help you discover your authentic self. (I have recommended a few of them in the Resources section at the end of the book.) Authenticity Advantage is different in that it will give you enough insight into six different aspects of yourself so that you can find who you really are. Only then can you discover what you really want.

I would love to tell you that I can make you more authentic; but to do that, you have to act on the knowledge you learn. Here is my promise: When you learn who you really are, you will be pleasantly surprised. When you realize you have a special GIFT, you will want to use it. When you see yourself the way God sees you, it will be the most awesome day of your life.

In the immortal words of Samuel Clemens, who wrote as Mark Twain:

> *The two most important days in your life are the day*
> *you were born and the day you find out why.*

I hope that as you discover your authentic self you will begin to develop it and to enjoy the abundant life for which you were created.

Chapter 2
Situation

As a brand-new Marine second lieutenant, I was taught that any time you prepare for a mission you should start by describing the situation. The two main components of the situation are the forces that the enemy has and the forces that you have. The same holds true for any project you start. Before you get started, it is a good idea to know what you are up against and what assets you have available.

What Are You Up Against?

The evidence that people are not acting from their authentic selves is everywhere. The problem is that experts who gather information fail to realize that many of the different labels they apply to polls and surveys are all just manifestations of the same root problem.

Gallup, Inc., published its *2020 State of the American Workplace: Employee Engagement Insights for US Business Leaders*. While their findings were a little better than in previous years, Gallup found that only 33% of employees are "engaged." Engaged employees work with passion and feel profound connection to their companies. They drive innovation and move organizations forward.

This statistic means that fully two-thirds of all employees are not engaged. Essentially, they are "checked out." These employees are sleepwalking through their workdays, putting in the time, but not the energy or passion. And some of them are actively disengaged employees. They aren't just unhappy at work; they're busy acting out their unhappiness. These are the kinds of workers who undermine what their engaged coworkers accomplish.

Gallup seems to target managers and leaders as the source of disengagement, and there is some evidence to support that claim. But could it be that Gallup targets managers and leaders because they represent a demographic that will pay for training to be more effective and productive in the workplace? How much of the issue really lies with the employees? If employees knew who they were and what they wanted, it follows that they would choose employment more aligned with their desires. Employees who are passionate about what they do will be more engaged at work. Managers can tap into that passion and help employees to be even more engaged, but is it really part of their jobs to find the passions of their employees?

A similar poll mentioned in Steven Covey's book, *The 8th Habit*, talks about the same issues. Covey cites a Harris poll of 23,000 US residents employed full time and compares it to a soccer team. I'm not much into soccer, so I have paraphrased the results and equated them to a football team.

If a football team had the same scores as the 23,000 employees in the poll:

◊ Only 4 of 11 players would know which goal was theirs.
◊ Only 2 of the 11 would care.
◊ Only 2 of the 11 would know what position they play and what they are supposed to do.
◊ And 9 players would be competing against their team members rather than the opponent.

While that might sound like something parents would see at a Pee Wee football game on a Saturday morning, it is a reality in many workplaces. So, whose fault is it? Managers or employees? Probably a little of both, but that's not really the issue.

The issue is that many of us take jobs or engage in careers we don't really like, or we work with people we don't really like, just to get a paycheck. Don't get me wrong, I'm all for getting a paycheck! What I'm not for, and what most people are not good with, is just surviving from paycheck to paycheck, year in and year out, with no end in sight, and with little fulfillment.

We want to be fulfilled. We want to be recognized for what we bring to the table. We want to be liked and loved for who we really are. But what happens when those needs are not met? What happens when we can't even express who we are or what we want? This reveals itself in the forms of stress and depression.

Stress

This might not go over well, but most of your stress is self-induced...and there is a lot of it. Much of the stress we feel is the result of comparison. We compare our worst selves to our perceptions of other people's best selves. If you use any form of social media, watch TV or movies, listen to podcasts, or read blogs you have probably fallen into this trap. All those forms of media portray people at their best, as if you should want what they are portraying.

The problem is that much of what you see, read, or hear has been manufactured; it isn't real. Many experts have proven that most of the social media photos and videos we think make people look so fantastic have been faked. That represents two problems: one for the person feeling they need to portray a fake image of themselves on social media to please others and one for those who look at those pictures and feel like a loser by comparison. An authentic person won't fall for either scenario.

We compare ourselves to what we think our parents expect. We compare ourselves to what we think our friends expect. We compare ourselves to what we think our spouses expect. Some of us compare ourselves to what we think God expects. Trying to live up to someone else's expectations will inevitably lead to stress.

Some of us try to impress people we don't even like by living a lifestyle we can't afford. Some of us portray a false image for people to whom we feel attracted. We'll buy clothes, cars, furniture, video equipment, computers, or houses to show others (and sometimes ourselves) how successful we are. But if you can't afford those things, it is called debt. Guess what being in debt causes? That's right... stress.

When under the burden of debt, giving up a job you don't like is not an option. And this is where many people find themselves—in debt. Whether the debt is from buying things you can't afford or the fact that you don't make enough money to last the month, it still causes stress. Even if you don't like your job, you know you need it, and you end up going to work every day in fear of losing the very thing you don't like. That's stress.

Many first-time employees enter the job market with huge student loans. That too is debt and another cause of stress. Whether you really needed to pay that much for college or not is an irrelevant question after the fact. The debt is real, and so is the stress.

Other causes of stress can be related to technology. How do you decompress on vacation (if you ever get to take one) when the calls, emails, and texts from work don't stop? If you have any level of responsibility in a career, the boundaries that used to be accepted, like the workday ended when you left the office, have disappeared. Many of us no longer even go to an office. That causes stress.

Dating used to be fun and an adventure. Now it is a business. If you can't find the right person in real life, then just find one online. No pressure there, right?

There is one more downside to technology. It is creating generations of very lonely people. Psychologists have dubbed the Millennial generation the "Loneliest Generation." Compared to previous generations, they are much less likely to have close, good, or best friends. When they need help to deal with the stresses of life, instead of turning to friends, family members, mentors, or pastors, Millennials are much more likely to get counseling from trained counselors. What was once regarded as something extreme is now considered "normal." That's stress.

What happens when stress is unresolved? Either physical illness or depression can occur. Many primary care physicians will tell you that the majority of the illnesses they treat can be directly attributed to stress. Depression, anxiety, eating disorders, obesity, type two diabetes, heart disease, hypertension, sexual dysfunction, sleep disorders, osteoporosis, alcoholism, PMS, and headaches have stress as a root cause.

Depression

One of the surest signs that so few people are authentic is the epidemic of depression in our population. According to the Anxiety and Depression Association of America, depression affects more than 15 million American adults, or about 6.7% of the US population ages 18 and older. (Can you believe there is such an organization? Now that's depressing.) Since 2013, Millennials have seen a 47% increase in major depression diagnoses. Both depression and "deaths of despair" (suicides) are on the rise and are linked to issues such as loneliness and stress about money.

According to an article in *Psychology Today*, the number one reason that Millennials are so depressed has to do with decision-making.[1] Between the ages of 25 and 35, people make major decisions that have lifelong consequences. This is when choices about getting married, buying houses, and having children are made, and many feel uncertain about how to make those decisions. They find that they have too many choices and that trying to distinguish between their options is overwhelming.

Suicide

First, some horrible facts about suicide. Between 1999 and 2016, the rate of suicide increased by 30%. It is the tenth leading cause of death in America. Each year, 44,192 Americans die by suicide; and for each death, 25 more attempt suicide. It costs the US $44 billion annually—not that it can be measured in dollars.

Approximately 58,000 Americans were killed in action in Vietnam, but the toll in suicides of the men and women who came home from that conflict is more than 100,000. (We don't know all the facts from the wars in Iraq and Afghanistan yet.) According to Suicide. org, untreated depression is the number one cause of suicide.

In the US military, there have been 45,000 suicides in the past six years, and the suicide rate for veterans is 1.5 times the rate of non-veterans. This is a severe problem that is being closely monitored.

Researchers asked 72 soldiers at one base why they tried to kill themselves; and out of the 33 reasons they had to choose from, all the soldiers included one reason in particular—a desire to end intense emotional distress.

When veterans who have survived suicide attempts are asked to describe what led them to this action, one of the top three reasons given is "feeling alone." The prevalence of suicidal thoughts appears to increase with the degree of loneliness.

I have heard experts on this subject speak before large audiences of police officers, who also share unusually high suicide rates. These experts' only solution to the devastating problem is what they call "awareness." Their solution is that if someone is aware that a person is having suicidal thoughts, then he or she can intervene to stop the suicidal act. While that's all well and good, does it solve the problem?

Pretending Is Exhausting

What do stress and depression have to do with one's Authenticity Advantage? EVERYTHING! As with depression, I would challenge anyone to find a person who knows his or her GIFT, purpose, and value to the world who would contemplate suicide. If anything, they would look for more time on the planet, not less.

The subtitle to *Use Your Authenticity Advantage* is *Because Pretending is Exhausting.* Stress is real, depression is real, and unfortunately so are suicidal thoughts. When you don't know who you really are—your authentic self—you will inevitably end up pretending to be someone you are not. That is exhausting because it is not natural.

The results of not being authentic, in addition to those already mentioned, include the constant struggles of tension, lack of enjoyment in life, worry about performance, having no one to confide in, gut problems and other illnesses, and a constant state of fear.

I hate to tell you this, but the odds are stacked against you. The "world" wants to keep you in this state of constant exhaustion and struggle. The "world" does that to keep you under its control. Have you noticed that communism and socialism all talk about the struggle of the working class? And the official book of National Socialism (the Nazis) is called *Mein Kampf*, which means "My Struggle." Anyone whose program is about your struggle fully intends to keep you there.

Your success does not depend on a government, political faction, company, or even religion. Your success is only found in your becoming who you were created to be. That requires authenticity.

What Are Your Assets?

Your personality, your unique way of thinking, your ability to master your emotions, your gender, and the unique way you were created to love are all assets of your authentic self. They are your Authenticity Advantage.

How do you decide on a career, a spouse, or a lifestyle when you don't know who you are or what you want? You don't. You either let someone else decide for you or you fake it and drift through life.

Sun Tzu, an ancient Chinese military strategist who wrote *The Art of War,* is often quoted by both military and business leaders. Sun Tzu once wrote:

> *If you know the enemy and know yourself, you need not fear the result of a hundred battles.*
> *If you know yourself but not the enemy, for every victory gained you will also suffer a defeat.*
> *If you know neither the enemy nor yourself, you will succumb in every battle.*

The purpose of describing a situation is to impress on you how important it is to know who you really are. Just knowing your authentic self gives you a 50/50 chance in battle. Even if you don't plan on going into battle anytime soon, being authentic gives you an advantage in getting ahead in whatever you choose. Without being authentic, you are very likely to fall prey to one of the two greatest enemies of your success: drifting and pretending.

Chapter 3
The Two Greatest Enemies

Drifting

Most people drift through life. By this, I mean that they go with the flow and accept whatever comes their way. It is as if life is a river, and the only option is to flow with the current. Drifting can be deceptively dangerous.

One of my duty stations in the Marine Corps was at the Marine Barracks in Washington, DC. The officers at the barracks were a pretty tight-knit group, and one spring weekend we decided to go on a whitewater rafting trip in West Virginia. A group of us arrived the day before our trek down the river and camped overnight.

The next morning, we rented two large inflatable rafts for six people each, and two smaller inflatable kayaks. I had one of the kayaks. The current wasn't too strong, and the water was calm for the first part of our trip. It didn't take long for all the Marines in the large rafts to become bored until someone had the bright idea to pretend to be a Viking raider. One raft bounced into the next raft, and then guys started boarding each other's Viking longboats (rafts) trying to throw people in the water. The two inflatable kayaks rammed the big rafts and pulled guys off to help the cause of their raiding party.

I should mention that we weren't the only ones rafting the river that day. The "civilians" on the river with us were shocked at first. Then they realized how much fun we were having. Needless to say, we provided a lot of entertainment for them on this boring part of the trip.

As we traveled closer to the whitewater portion of the river, everyone got back in their rafts, I mean Viking longboats, and prepared for the rough water. Getting through the rapids turned into a race to see who could get through the fastest. After the last inflatable raft made it through the rapids, we paddled up on shore. Then the rafting company drove us back upstream to the camp ground. It was all great fun.

So, what's the point?

Rafts drifting down a river is an analogy for how some go through life. The river represents a strong force that one cannot overcome; and if you try to paddle against the flow, all you get is exhaustion. So, the only option becomes going with the flow. You can drift and have fun, or you can drift and be bored. You can do it with others or by yourself. You can participate in the fun or be entertained by others drifting with you. Regardless, you have little to no control over where you end up. It all depends on the river.

What happens if the current becomes too strong? What happens when the rapids become extremely violent? Or, what happens if the river goes over a cliff? You and all the other drifters could perish. But what can you do about it? You have no control.

This is exactly how many people feel. They feel there is some invisible force that makes everyone go in the same direction, and they feel powerless to fight that system. The best they can hope for is to enjoy the ride, be entertained, or maybe have a little nicer raft than the other guy. How long the ride lasts or how bumpy it becomes seem out of their control. What can they do about it?

You can tell someone is drifting by their language. They say things like, "another day, another dollar" or "made it through another week." They sarcastically say they are "living the dream" when you know they are not. Drifters are also infamous for saying, "It is what it is." "Whatever," another favorite expression, was voted "the most annoying word in a conversation" in college polls of 2009 and 2010. All these terms denote a sense of indifference and apathy. Why? Because these people are drifting.

Drifting is the opposite of purpose. It leads to hopelessness, helplessness, and depression. Since drifters find no purpose in their lives, everything seems to be a matter of luck or chance to them. There doesn't seem to be a meaning for anything. That can lead to abuse.

> ***When purpose is not known,***
> ***abuse is inevitable.***
> ***~Myles Munroe***

No one wants to be without hope, and very few people tolerate feeling helpless and out of control. To suppress those emotions, many people will turn to amusements to take their minds off the source of their pain or frustration. The word *amuse*, from which we get amusement, has a very interesting origin. *Muse* means to reflect, ponder, meditate, or be absorbed in thought. These are all activities that drifters avoid with passion. *Amuse,* means the opposite. It means to deceive and cheat by occupying and diverting your attention. The more you seek amusements, the more you are drifting through life.

Pretending

The second greatest enemy of your success is pretending to be who or what you are not. It is as if you put on a mask to make people see something different than your true self. If you wear the mask too long, you can begin to forget who you really are.

My parents were both extroverts. Dad was a loud, gregarious, Marine first sergeant and the patriarch of our extended family.

Mom was a professional ice skater who loved being the center of attention. I had great parents and wanted to be just like them. The problem was that my personality and theirs were nothing alike. So, I tried to change mine. Florence Littauer calls that "wearing a mask" in her book *Your Personality Tree.*

From the time I was in high school until I was in my late thirties, I tried to wear the mask of someone who was a confident, extroverted leader. I went to parties and bars with the boys only to look for the exit within 15 minutes of arriving. I politely listened to their raunchy jokes, only to think they weren't funny. I gave orders that my subordinates had to obey without knowing how to inspire people to follow. I had to learn how to be both social and inspirational. It did not come naturally, and it was hard work. That is a sign that I was wearing a mask.

The entire time I was wearing a mask, I was completely unaware that was what I was doing. I just knew that nothing came easily. All that changed when I took a DISC personality assessment. The kind of assessment I took, and the kind I will recommend to you in a later chapter, provided me with two different profiles. It showed my natural personality and my environmental personality. Basically, by looking at both profiles, I could see how I was masking my real (natural) personality at work to compensate for my perception of what was required. I was trying to be an extroverted dominant, directing, doer type person (something the DISC personality assessment calls a D personality) only to find that the three best words to describe my personality were cold, critical, and aloof. You can probably guess I was not happy with my assessment, even though I had to agree with it.

That's when I asked a really good question. I said out loud, "Okay God, you made me this way…why?" Then I heard a still, small voice reply, "It is about time you asked the right question." That was the moment I started to accept who I really was. There was a reason I was the way I was, and wearing a mask was never going to take me where God intended. I was relieved to know there was an easier, more natural way.

In her book, Florence Littauer describes several situations of people wearing masks. She writes:

> *Fun-loving children were forced to get serious and keep quiet, while introverts were told to put on a happy face to be popular. Born leaders were disciplined into an unnatural submission and those who would rather watch were pushed into leadership.*

Regardless of what mask you might wear, it isn't natural, it isn't fun, it's hard work…in fact, it is exhausting! You will not have an Authenticity Advantage until you can identify your mask and take it off. Your advantage lies in the real you.

Chapter 4
What It Means to Be Authentic

Throughout the following pages, I'll talk about authenticity and being authentic, so it is a good idea to define those words to make sure there are no misconceptions.

Authenticity is the quality of being authentic. Various dictionaries define *authentic* as real or genuine; not false or imitation; true to one's own personality, spirit, or character; of an undisputed origin; and being without deceit or hypocrisy.

Terms used to describe authenticity	Terms describing things NOT authentic
Real	Fake
Genuine	Counterfeit
Trustworthy	Untrustworthy
Valid	Invalid
Legitimate	Illegitimate
True	False
Credible	Corrupt
Reliable	Unreliable
Sincere	Deceitful
Operates by love, hope, and purpose	Operates by fear, anxiety, and drifting

Authenticity carries with it a sense of relaxed confidence that comes from being true to who you really are.

People who are authentic share these characteristics:

◊ They are honest about their feelings.

◊ They know they can't please everyone, so they don't try.

◊ They live their own lives instead of comparing themselves to others.

◊ They tell the truth.

◊ They are honest.

◊ They know who they are, so they don't pretend to be someone they're not.

◊ They live in the moment with a positive expectation for the future.

◊ They make their own decisions.

◊ They acknowledge their own mistakes.

◊ They celebrate the successes of others.

◊ They trust their intuition.

◊ They put a value on the experiences of life, not on possessions.

◊ They give love and respect freely.

◊ They are open-minded.

◊ They associate with uplifting people.

Because of these characteristics, authentic people are a pleasure to be around. You never have to guess where they are coming from, and they can accept you for who you really are. You can intuitively feel that they only want to give you something, and without an ulterior motive. Associating with authentic people is a breath of fresh air in a chaotic world.

> ### *Associating with authentic people is a breath of fresh air in a chaotic world.*

One of the main advantages of becoming an authentic person is that you will attract people to you. Who wouldn't want to be around someone who doesn't criticize you and with whom you don't have to keep your guard up? The authentic person gets to hear the truth from others rather than just hearing what others think you want to hear.

Jesus said, "...you will know the truth, and the truth will make you free." A non-authentic person will rarely hear the truth or recognize the truth when it is spoken. Attracting people to you, especially the ones who speak the truth, is an invaluable asset in becoming successful in any field of endeavor.

In the words of a *Forbes* article written by Travis Bradberry:

> *Genuine (authentic) people know who they are. They are confident enough to be comfortable in their own skin. They are firmly grounded in reality, and they're truly present in each moment because they're not trying to figure out someone else's agenda or worrying about their own.*[2]

Authenticity Is an Inside-Out Job

Being authentic has to do with one's character, not their outward appearance. As you read through some of the words that describe someone who may not be authentic in the chart above, you might immediately think of people who try to change themselves from the outside in. I am all for trying to look your best, but a tummy tuck, a facelift, breast implants, or taking steroids so your muscles look bigger does nothing to change who you are on the inside. Those kinds of things have the opposite effect. They enhance a false image of who one really is.

I am not saying that we should not try to look our best, but if you are trying to make a radical change to your exterior you should ask yourself why. Are you trying to look younger or older? Are you trying to look more athletic? Do you change your hair color or eye color in an attempt to change your persona? Why does your persona need to change?

Superficial changes may seem to make a difference, but only temporarily. You still know the issues you are struggling with. Others may be attracted to the "new you," but only until they discover the person inside…and they will.

When you are authentic at your core, your outside will become more attractive. It is not about improving your body; it is about being who you really are on the inside. I am going to deal with this in more depth later, but the real you, the one you are trying to mask, is perfect. You just may not know that person yet.

God does not make mistakes; and no, you are not an exception. The right people will warm up and be attracted to the real you. The people you are trying to attract by not being authentic either shy away from you because they can tell you are pretending to be what you are not, or they are not the people with whom you should associate. Your personality and your GIFT are perfect for you, and others will think so as well.

Why Authenticity Is Important

In a recent article in *Psychology Today*, Tchiki Davis made some interesting observations. She said:

> *I'm now convinced that it's harder for us to be our true selves now, in the technology age. We are constantly bombarded with media that tells us who to be, what to want, and how we "should" express ourselves. All*

of these influences slowly chip away at our ability to be our authentic selves...

We were molded as children by our parents, teachers, religions, peers, and society to "fit in." As a result, we developed beliefs, thoughts, emotions, and behaviors that keep us acting in the ways we were taught to act—not in the ways that make us feel like our authentic selves.

This version of ourselves can be thought of as the "Adaptive Self"...if you're feeling inauthentic, the Adaptive Self is running your life.[3]

What Dr. Davis calls your "Adaptive Self" is the non-authentic version of you. Your Adaptive Self took years to develop, and it was insidious. By that, I mean that it happened very gradually, and it was probably subconscious. You didn't even realize it was happening. For most of us, myself included, this non-authentic version of ourselves becomes our reality. We wonder why everything seems so difficult, so much work, and feels like drudgery. The good news is that it doesn't have to stay that way.

The answer lies in becoming your authentic self. It means pursuing your own goals, doing things your way, and finding your purpose. Your authentic self and your purpose are not hard to identify or let out. You just need to know how to do it. So, stay tuned.

Let's Get Honest

The first step in discovering your authentic self so that you can leverage your Authenticity Advantage is to get brutally honest with yourself. I say "brutally" honest to stress there can be no compromise here. You need to be aware of your real starting point. If you lie to yourself here, it will not produce the results you deserve.

Anytime you use your GPS to find out how long it will take to drive somewhere, you need two vital bits of information. You must know your starting point and your destination. If you input that information incorrectly, the predicted time of your trip will not be correct. For example, if I want to drive to Disney World in Florida, I have to tell Google Maps or the GPS in my car where I want to start and where I want to go.

I live in North Carolina. For the sake of this example, let's say I want to drive to Charleston, South Carolina, to visit some friends and then drive to Disney World. I want to know how long it will take me to drive from Charleston to the Disney Resort. So, I type in my starting point as Charleston and my destination as Disney World. The only problem is, unknown to me, the first Charleston that comes up in my search is for Charleston, West Virginia, not Charleston, South Carolina. My results show the drive to be 12 hours and 2 minutes. The actual drive from Charleston, South Carolina, is 6 hours and 2 minutes. That's a six-hour difference. This is why knowing your starting point is so important.

Your starting point is knowing who you really are, and your destination is knowing what you want. Most people don't honestly know either of those points of reference. It is not comfortable to admit you don't know the real you, especially if you have been pretending to be someone else for a while. You have established habits and acquaintances based on this false self and it may seem more comfortable to just keep things as they are.

The problem is that you may have a nagging feeling that something is missing. You may have asked yourself, "Is this it? Is this all there is to life? Why do I feel so empty and unfulfilled? I have no value, and no one would even miss me if I disappeared." First, if you have asked yourself any of those questions, please realize you are not alone. But those questions are just symptoms of not knowing who you really are, and the real you is awesome!

If you don't know who you really are, and that's almost everyone, then there is no way you can know what you want. It is not possible. This is the biggest reason most people have no idea what their purpose is and why they aren't even looking for it. What you want, as opposed to what you may think you want, is a desire that comes from knowing your special GIFT. But again, you cannot find your GIFT without knowing who you really are.

Once you know who you really are, then finding your GIFT becomes possible. Employing your GIFT is your purpose, and you will have a natural desire to use it. Then finding what you want to do and what you want to have becomes easy. The challenge is that most people have not been taught any of this.

You have probably been taught that you needed to get good grades in school so you could go to college. With the right college degree, you could get a good job. Then you could work the job until age 65 so you could retire. After retirement, you can live freely and do all the things you wanted to do, but couldn't when you had a job. This plan requires that you trade your time for money so that you can enjoy your time with the money you have earned, at least until the money runs out.

There are a few problems with that plan. A college degree does not necessarily turn into a good job or career. A good job or career does not mean you can save enough for retirement. In fact, most Americans do not have enough in their bank accounts to cover a $500 emergency. Those that do retire spend most of their time worrying about if they have enough money to last them until they die. Nowhere in any of this plan is any consideration given to using your GIFT and being all you were created to be.

There is a better plan, one based on your Authenticity Advantage. For this plan to work you need to answer three questions.

1. Who are you?
   ◊ Not who do you think you are
   ◊ Not who do others say you are
   ◊ Not who do you want to become
2. What do you want to do?
   ◊ Not what did you make up to tell everyone
   ◊ Not what do your parents want you to do
   ◊ Not what does your spouse want you to do
3. What do you want to have?
   ◊ Not what society or advertisements tell you to want
   ◊ Not what you want to look good to others
   ◊ Not what you want to distract you from thinking about what matters most

The answers to questions 2 and 3 stem, or should stem, from who you really are. The answer to question number 1 is the foundation from which all your other answers flow naturally.

Zig Ziglar, one of the best-known personalities of the personal development industry, is famous for this quote:

> ### *You have to BE before you can DO and DO before you can HAVE.*

In other words, having is the result of being and doing.

Unfortunately, most of us have been taught differently. Our educational system teaches us to prepare to DO. You may have taken a skills or aptitude assessment in high school to point you in a potential career direction. The military uses the ASVAB test to do this as well. But just because you have an aptitude for something doesn't mean you will find it fulfilling, does it? It only means you can do it. This leads many to only consider what they can do to make a dollar, with little or no consideration of what they desire.

On the other hand, people who are entrepreneurially oriented often speak of what they want to HAVE. They then figure out what they must do to get what they want. Again, fulfillment and purpose take a back seat to other considerations.

For those looking to be authentic, you must buck conventional wisdom that says to start by doing. Instead. begin by knowing who you are. As Zig Ziglar so aptly put it, who you are will determine what you do, and what you do will determine what you have. This is the only true course to having a fulfilled life.

I Learned the Hard Way

Learning that I was supposed to BE before doing did not come easily to me. The career I chose after college was in the military. I wanted to be a pilot, not because I had any great aeronautical gift, but because I thought it would be cool. And if I was going to be a military pilot, I wanted to do it in the Marine Corps. Why? Just because I wanted to prove I could do it. How is that for great career advice?

Twelve years later I decided I chose the wrong profession, and it was time to find out what I was really supposed to do with my life. I thoroughly enjoyed my time in the Marine Corps, and I was pretty good at my job, but it just wasn't "it" for me. You know, "it" is what you were born to do. By the way, the twelve-year mark is not typically when people decide to leave the military. Most leave after their obligation is fulfilled, which would have been at five years of service for me, or after they reach retirement eligibility at 20 years of service. But I had to be different. I had to find "it."

I left the Marines with no real plan or job...and without a pension. That was bad enough, but that's also when I discovered I had no idea who I was. As a Marine pilot, my entire identity was wrapped up in my career. It determined the clothes I wore, the friends I hung out with, and to a large degree led me to my wife. The car I drove, the vacations we took, the house we lived in, the town we lived in, and even the movies I watched were all influenced by my career. Last, but not least, it determined my purpose. As a Marine officer, it was eminently clear that my purpose was to defend the nation against its enemies, and I was proud to do it.

If someone asked me who I was, I would have told them I was a Marine pilot without hesitation. To me, that said it all. If I was in uniform, my rank and pilot wings told people who I was. If I was wearing normal clothes my haircut, my demeanor, and the decals on my car gave me away.

But then I took the uniform off, and everything changed. I was no longer Major Gilroy. I was just another guy trying to find a job and starting all over again. I didn't know what I wanted to do, and I didn't know what I could have. I never even thought about money when I was a Marine because the pay was what it was, and all my friends made the same amount as I did. I no longer had purpose, and money became paramount. What was I supposed to do?

Some of you can readily identify with this if you have had to transition from the military. But no matter your profession, everyone will lose their job eventually. You will either change careers, change companies, be downsized (fired), or retire. That's when you get to find out who you really are…if you haven't already.

My point is this: You are not your career, job, profession, or even ministry. In fact, that is exactly backwards. What you do should be a reflection of who you are. So, if your job defines you, as mine did, you may not know the real you. It is very worthwhile to make the effort to find out who you really are.

Advantage

Normally when someone refers to having an advantage (as in an Authenticity Advantage) it means that you have a position or condition of superiority in order to achieve success. Without even saying it, the mere possession of an advantage implies competition.

Anyone who lives and works in the world realizes that we compete for almost anything that is worthwhile. We compete for a mate, we compete for grades in school, we compete in sports, and we compete in our careers, which means we compete for income. Whether we like it or not is irrelevant. Competition is the rule; and when competing, we always look for an advantage. If we didn't have competition, success and achievement would have little joy.

For the most part, competition is what drives progress. But some people become obsessed with competition. They will go to extremes to win, forsaking the rules and ethics of society. For some, competition means winning at all costs. To them, an advantage is anything they can use to beat their opponents; and whether it is legal or illegal, ethical or unethical, does not matter to them.

To be clear, that is not what I mean by your Authenticity Advantage. Actually, your Authenticity Advantage implies that by not being authentic, you are actually placing yourself at a disadvantage. Since everyone has an Authenticity Advantage, using your advantage puts you on an even playing field. Where before you may have found the game of life to be a struggle, now it becomes fun. And competition? Well, that spurs you on to become better at playing the game.

Chapter 5
Who Are You Really?

What a great question! In fact, it is a question people have been asking for millennia. Here are just a few quotes on the subject:

> *"For as he thinks within himself, so is he."*
> *—Solomon, Proverbs, circa 950 BC*

> *"Know Thyself."*
> *—Socrates, circa 400 BC*

> *"This above all: to thine own self be true...."*
> *—Shakespeare, Hamlet, circa 1600 AD*

> *"I think, therefore I am."*
> *—Descartes, Discourse on Method, 1637*

> *"The two most important days in your life are the day you are born and the day you find out why."*
> *—Samuel Clemmons, circa 1860*

> *"Today you are you! That is truer than true! There is no one alive who is you-er than you!"*
> *—Dr. Seuss, Happy Birthday to You!, 1959*

Do you think about who you really are? According to Heidi Grant Halvorson in a *Psychology Today article*:

> *Trying to figure it all out on your own is close to im-*

possible. Relying on our intuitions alone for self-knowl-edge is dangerous, because thanks to the nature of the adaptive unconscious, they are often no more accurate than a shot in the dark.[4]

So, two points to take away from this quote are:
1. The importance of knowing yourself is well established.
2. Trying to figure it out based on your intuition is worthless.

If you assume for a second that you don't know the real, authentic you, how do you find it? One person might tell you that your personality is the answer. Another might say that your strengths are what really define you. An expert might tell you to analyze where your thoughts are formed. Your pastor might tell you that God will reveal it to you. Best of all, your friends may tell you it doesn't matter, so don't worry about it.

How can you tell which answer is right? Many different books, assessments, and methods of determining the real you have value, but just singling out one of them will only give you an incomplete picture of your authentic self.

There is no one method or answer to discovering who you really are. However, if you combine the results of a few proven assessments of what makes you the unique person you are, you will get a much more complete picture than if you try to figure it out on your own. This section will help you to know the real you so that you can become more authentic.

3-Part Person

Whether you realize it or not, there are actually three parts of your being. You are a spirit, who has a soul, which resides in a body.

Your body is the physical being that other people see. They recognize you because of your face, your hair, your eyes…you get the point. It is precisely because your body is how other people recognize you that many people only consider this aspect of who they are. They are more concerned with their weight, their physique, and their age than the more important aspects of who they are.

When I speak of your authenticity, I am not referring to a physical attribute. In other words, I am not referring to how beautiful you are, how fast you can run, or how well you use your hands as a mechanic. While those things may give you a competitive edge, it would be a mistake to call any physical attribute your Authenticity Advantage.

On the other extreme is the part of you that is spirit. Many people have no concept of the fact that they are spirit-beings, and it is not my intention to convince anyone of that fact. I only bring it up because those of you who do recognize your spirit-being may interpret your authenticity as a purely spiritual thing. I believe that supernatural gifts do exist, and they do relate to the way I describe your authentic self, but they are not what I refer to when I describe your Authenticity Advantage.

Your soul is distinct from your body and your spirit. It is a combination of your mind, your will, and your emotions. Your soul plays a part in who you are as a person with a body and as a spirit. Your soul is completely unique to you, and you have complete control over it. Just as your body is unique as identified by your fingerprints, your retinal scan, and your DNA; so is your way of thinking completely unique.

My point is that when I refer to your authenticity, I am referring to a part of your soul. As I discuss the different aspects of who you really are, I will primarily focus on your unique way of thinking. Here is why.

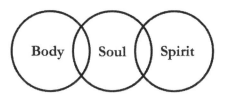

Diagram 1

Diagram 1 shows a relationship between the three parts that make up your being. Notice that they are interconnected, with your soul being in the middle. A person's soul (what we refer to as our mind, will, and emotions) is influenced by both our body and our spirit.

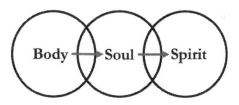

Diagram 2

Our soul is most often influenced by our body as shown in Diagram 2. What we see, hear, smell, taste, and touch affects our thinking, our emotions, and our decisions. However, these are under your control, and your soul is where that control is exerted. It is in your soul that thinking occurs, decisions are made, and your personality resides.

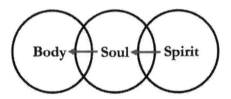

Diagram 3

Diagram 3 shows that your spirit cannot affect your body without going through your soul, which is one of the reasons that St. Paul says we need to "renew" our minds. More to the point of your Authenticity Advantage, if you want to make a lasting change to your physical appearance, your relationships, or your income, it is critical to renew your thinking. *Renew* is an interesting choice of words because it means to take your thinking back to its original condition, before the world and all its influences corrupted what and how you think.

As you will soon discover, how you think is the most unique aspect of who you really are. It is an aspect to which most people pay very little attention; but it is completely under your control, and it can be your greatest Authenticity Advantage.

Six Aspects of Who You Are

When people talk about you, what do they say? No, I don't mean what gossip they might be spreading, but how do they describe you? Is it by what you do for a job? Is it by your role in a family? Is it by your age and gender? Do any of those descriptions provide an accurate picture of the real you?

What do you say about yourself? If someone asked you who you are, how would you reply? Could you answer immediately, or would you have to think about it? Would your answer depend on the circumstances? Mine did. My answer was tied directly to my profession until I learned what I am about to show you.

When I conduct a seminar, I'll ask people to take out a piece of paper and I give them 15 seconds to fill in the blank.

I am _____.

How would you answer that question? Could you do it in 15 seconds? The way you answer is quite revealing. If you are at all unsure of your answer, or you must think about it, you are subconsciously sending mixed signals to those you meet. If you don't know how to describe yourself, then the people you meet won't be able to tell who you are either.

On the other hand, if you can answer quickly, but your answer is wrong because you are wearing a mask and pretending to be someone you are not, then they will treat you like the person you pretend to be…sort of. I say "sort of" because people have an uncanny knack for telling when someone is not being genuine with them.

How you answer this simple, yet profound question is the basis of your relationships. Being authentic allows people to know how to react to you. You will find that the right people will be attracted to your authentic self, and those you are not meant to have a relationship with will naturally keep their distance. The confidence you have in who you really are will put people at ease and remove a lot of stress in your life.

How you fill in the blank of I am _____ requires some introspection and reflection. There are so many different aspects of the complex person that is you, that it could take volumes to describe you. In fact, you may already be aware of numerous volumes and methodologies that attempt to describe the real you.

To keep things simple and to help you get a clear understanding of the wonderful person you are, I have chosen six aspects for you to study about yourself. Even if you have a good idea of who you are now, by the time you are finished looking at these six aspects you will gain a new appreciation of yourself. You might even fill in the blank differently when you are done.

The six aspects we will explore are:

1. Personality
2. Gender
3. Generation
4. How you think about money
5. How you give and receive love
6. GIFT

As I explain each of these aspects, you will discover that they provide insight into how you think. Each aspect has a profound influence on who you are, and together they will give you an Authenticity Advantage.

1. Personality

Most parents who have more than one child will tell you their children are very different from each other, and they noticed the differences soon after birth.

Merriam-Webster's Collegiate Dictionary contains this interesting definition of *personality*: "The complex of characteristics that distinguishes an individual or a nation or a group; the totality of an individual's behavioral and emotional tendencies; the organization of the individual's distinguishing character traits, attitudes or habits."

How you act, react, organize, and form habits is based on your personality. Or to put it another way, how you behave is primarily influenced by your personality.

You were born with your personality. Each person's personality is perfect for him or her. No one personality type is better than another. You can hide your real personality behind a mask, you can then unmask it, but you cannot change how you were created.

Since your personality affects the way you act, how you react to circumstances, how you organize your thoughts, how you form habits, and how you think about things, wouldn't it be a good idea to understand your personality as well as you can?

Recalling my not so well-planned exit from the military, one of the reasons I had such a hard time finding what I was supposed to do for a career was because I had no idea who I was as a person.

My dad was a Marine first sergeant when I was a kid. He was loud, outgoing, well respected, and well liked. Dad was also the patriarch of our extended family. Whenever an aunt, uncle, or cousin had a problem, they called Dad. He loved children, animals, and almost all people. He was my hero and the person I tried to model my personality after. That presented a problem.

Unlike my father, I was shy, reserved, quiet, and hated crowds. Trying to fit in was a constant struggle, mostly because behaving like my dad did not work for me. I did well in school and sports, not so much because I was competitive or well liked (which I wasn't), but because I worked hard. I did it to make my dad proud. He never asked that of me or even hinted I needed to do anything to gain his approval. As far as Dad was concerned, I had his approval just because I was his son. All my pressure was self-induced.

As a senior in high school, I applied for a Navy ROTC scholarship and admission to the University of Virginia. While at the university, I switched my scholarship to the Marines, and I applied for an aviation guarantee that would allow me to be pre-approved for flight school after graduating. After flight school, I got my first choice of duty station and aircraft. I had no idea how competitive any of those choices were.

When I checked in to my first squadron, I found myself in the company of some of the most aggressive and competitive men in America, without even realizing I was essentially engaged in a competition. Traits of leadership, physical and mental courage, and ethical behavior were expected of Marine officers, as were characteristics of being dominant, directing, take-charge doers. Any weaknesses detected by your brother pilots could be fatal to your career. Most of those behaviors did not come naturally to me; I had to learn them. Everything about a career as a Marine pilot was hard work for me.

Even though I did well, I never felt like I fit in. I didn't like going to bars, I wasn't a ladies' man, and I wasn't into all the macho stuff. Don't get me wrong, I had a lot of fun and enjoyed being a Marine even though I wasn't your typical flyboy.

I did that for 12 years. I was proud of my accomplishments and proud to wear the uniform. What I didn't realize was how much of my real self I had been masking. I learned to be a leader. I learned to be a skilled pilot. I learned people skills. None of those things came naturally to me, so it was no wonder that my frustration level continued to rise with my rank. I had no idea who I really was or that I was covering up the real me.

Only after leaving the Marine Corps and discovering the personal development industry did things change. Taking a personality assessment literally changed my life.

Personality Assessments

Several institutions have developed excellent methods for testing and categorizing personalities. The one I first took, and still recommend, is the DISC personality assessment.

I had been trained to be an aggressive leader. The person I admired most, my dad, was loud, gregarious, and loved people; so I tried to mold my personality into those characteristics. My DISC assessment showed me why that was a problem. Instead of being a charismatic influencer of people, able to direct them to accomplish great tasks, my profile said something radically different. The three words that best described my personality according to my DISC assessment were *cold*, *critical*, and *aloof*. Doesn't sound too charismatic, does it? And as far as loving people like my dad did, well that didn't show up in the assessment either.

The problem is that the assessment was accurate. When I got really honest with myself, that is exactly how I felt…almost. I agreed with the cold and critical part, but not the aloof part. That was because I didn't know what aloof meant. I had to look it up. In case you don't know the meaning of aloof either, it means distant and not friendly, standoffish. I knew I felt that way and went to great lengths to cover it up and not let others see how I really felt.

Discovering that my natural behavior was completely different from what I wanted it to be was quite a shock. But I couldn't argue with the results. Finally, I went to God and asked Him why He made me this way. Until then I had complained to Him about myself, like there was something wrong with me. I didn't complain out loud or to other people, and I wasn't depressed either. I just wondered why I couldn't seem to be the loving person my dad was.

My DISC assessment taught me there was nothing wrong with my personality…it was just different (a fact my wife can attest to). I had to unlearn who I thought I was and start becoming who I was created to be. Now the journey truly began.

The reason I recommend DISC over other personality assessments is because it is designed for individuals. It can be used by companies to see if employees are a good fit for the organization, something the other assessments seem primarily focused on, but DISC is well adapted to an individual who wants to develop personally or professionally.

The DISC personality assessment is relatively easy to understand. There are only four major personality types to explain. Your blend of those four types helps to explain your particular personality, with the basic style chart of that blend showing how you naturally behave.

There is one other feature about DISC assessments that bears some discussion. The version of DISC I recommend in the Resources section will provide you with two different personality profiles. One is based on your environment, and it may change over time. The other is your natural profile, which does not change. The more these two profiles are similar, the more likely you are doing something that is a natural fit for you. In other words, it demonstrates how authentic you are while on the job. This information could be a game changer for you, as it was for me.

Your personality isn't the only aspect of who you really are, but it is a big indicator. If you have never taken a personality assessment for yourself, as opposed to being a requirement for a job, I strongly recommend it. Why would you guess when you can know?

> ***The more you can behave like your natural "real" self, the faster you will be able to work from your strengths.***

2. Gender

This is not as touchy a subject as you might assume. (Remember, the point of this book is to help you find your Authenticity Advantage.)

Hopefully, you have already come to realize that how you think is affected by your unique personality and that everyone doesn't think like you. Your gender affects how you think as well.

Did you know that scientists have discovered 100 differences between male and female brains? I learned this from a *Psychology Today* article published by Gregory L. Jantz.[5] Men have seven times more gray matter than women and have information and action processing centers in specific "boxes" in a specific area of the brain. Men can have tunnel vision when they are doing something, so once they are concentrating on a task or game, they probably won't show too much sensitivity to other people or even be aware of their surroundings. (I can hear you ladies laughing in agreement.)

On the other hand, women have 10 times more white matter than their male counterparts. White matter is the networking grid that connects the brain's gray matter and other processing centers with one another. It is the reason girls tend to transition more quickly between tasks than boys. It is also the reason why females are great multi-taskers, while men excel in highly task-focused projects.

When I listen to two women talking, I'm amazed at how they can follow each other. Shifting a conversation from one subject to another and then back again is natural to them. That's because everything is connected to everything else in the female brain. I often have to stop my wife in mid-sentence and ask her if we just changed subjects. Her reply is usually something pithy like, "Just keep up."

Females have verbal centers on both sides of the brain while males only have verbal centers in the left hemisphere. There are also chemical differences that make men less inclined to sit still for as long as females and make them tend to be more physically impulsive and aggressive than women.

Guys, here is a warning: If your best girl says she wants to talk about a problem, she probably isn't looking for you to solve it for her. She probably just wants to talk. I know it doesn't make sense to you, but it does to her…doesn't it, ladies? She'll let you know if she needs your help.

So, while it might not be politically correct, when it comes to who you are, scientifically speaking, your gender does make a difference. Of course, most of you already knew that, even if you didn't know the science behind it.

3. Generation

Because we are living longer, we now have four very different generations in the workforce all at the same time. The benefit is that we have four generational perspectives on the challenges of today. The problem is that we have four generational perspectives on the challenges of today. Depending on your generation, you could be excited or exasperated.

Let's start by defining the different generations. They are:
◊ **Traditional**—after the "Greatest Generation (WWII)" but before Baby Boomers. Only a few of this generation are still working
◊ **Baby Boomers**
◊ **Gen X**—also called "latchkey kids"
◊ **Millennials**—also called Gen Y and net Gen (I also include Generation Z with the Millennials. While there are significant differences in Millennials and Zs, there hasn't been enough research on Zs to make an accurate statement about how they think.)

Each generation has major differences in how they act, communicate, and think. The following chart helps to define some of those for the three dominant generations in the workforce.

Baby Boomer (75 million)	Gen X (66 million)	Gen Y / net Gen / Millennial (largest generation)
Born 1945–1964	Born 1964–1982	Graduate HS in 2000
Industrial Age	Transition Era	Information Age
Traditional	Independent	Work in Groups
Optimistic about Future	"Whatever"	Pessimistic about Future
Call	Email	TXT

The Baby Boomer generation represents a huge population, roughly 75 million. They were born between 1945 and 1964. They grew up in the Industrial Age—a time before computers and cell phones. Most of today's management theory is still based on Baby Boomers' thinking, which values the bottom line and believes workers are numbers that can be replaced. If you've ever been told to do something "because I said so" or because "that's how we've always done it," chances are you are hearing it from an Industrial Age Baby Boomer. They still represent a large number of business owners and corporate managers.

Baby Boomers are known for their more traditional values. When they were growing up, the assault on fatherhood hadn't fully hit. They expected to do better than their parents and were told the key to getting ahead was more education. Their preferred method of communicating is either face to face or on the phone. They grew up with TV shows like *Gunsmoke, Leave It to Beaver*, and *The Andy Griffith Show*.

Generation X is a transition generation. They were caught between the Industrial Age and the Information Age. They weren't born in a world with computers and the internet, but they learned to use them as tools. Their generation numbers about 66 million, and they were born between 1964 and 1982.

Generation X was taught to be independent. Their Baby Boomer parents were so engaged in their careers that many Gen Xers were left to take care of themselves. That is how they acquired the nickname "latchkey kids." It comes from the fact that many in this generation had their own house key because they needed it to unlock the door when they got home from school since both parents were still at work. They didn't have parents hovering over their every move, so they became very independent.

If there is a word that describes a person from Generation X it would be "whatever," and they are not as driven to succeed as their predecessors. Their favorite mode of communication is email, but they have adapted to texting and social media. They are not as optimistic as the Baby Boomer generation, preferring to go with the flow. They came of age watching *Friends* and *Seinfeld* on TV.

The Millennial generation is projected to surpass the huge Baby Boom generation as the nation's largest living generation, according to population projections released by the US Census Bureau. They were born after 1982 and grew up with computers and the internet. They were also schooled differently than previous generations, being taught to work in groups to gather information for projects.

Their expectations are remarkably different from previous generations. They expect to do worse economically than their parents, but they expect a job to come with a college degree. They also tend to communicate via social media and texting rather than have social interaction face to face or on the phone.

A story about the perceptions of two different generations in the same workplace makes the point. On a flight from Chicago to Washington, DC, I was seated between two young Millennial women. I had just read an article in a newspaper about the attitudes and work ethic of the Millennial generation. The cover story picture showed a young woman in casual attire and flip-flops sitting on top of a desk in an office room. Not exactly the traditional work environment I am used to. So, I asked my two Millennial seatmates what they thought of the article. They immediately conferred with each other (they were total strangers) and then told me they agreed with what the author of the article had said about the way Millennials work compared to previous generations.

Suddenly, the oxygen masks popped out of the ceilings over our seats. My first thought was, *Wow, that's unusual.* To my great surprise, no one screamed or acted crazy. The pilot came on the loudspeaker and said we had lost cabin pressure but there was nothing else wrong with the airplane. We ended up making a precautionary landing in Cincinnati. This meant I had more time to talk with the two women. It was very educational.

When I finally returned to my office in Chicago, I gathered all the Millennials in the office to ask their opinion of the *USA Today* article. I told them what the two women on the airplane said and asked if they agreed. The conversation soon became loud and excited. They couldn't believe how I thought, and they were amazed that a Baby Boomer listened to them. The conversation centered around "why."

Almost every time I would ask one of them to do something they would ask, "Why?" To my way of thinking this was insubordinate and just being stubborn. What I didn't realize was why they were asking "why." Millennials are part of the Information Age. Through computers, the internet, cell phones, and a host of other technology, they are used to gathering all the pertinent information they can before beginning a project. When they are asking "why" it is so that they can gather the correct information. I learned this from my two Millennial flying companions and was eager to see if my co-workers thought the same way.

As the discussion in our office progressed, the CEO came storming out of his office. We all thought he was angry. Well, he was certainly emotional, but he wasn't angry with any of us. It turned out that he had been recently "challenged" by his son with a "why" question. Overhearing our conversation, the CEO now understood that his son's "challenge" wasn't a challenge at all. Everyone had a good laugh, and the communication in that office rose to a new level.

What's the point? The point is that new generations come to maturity every 10 to 20 years. Your generation is a part of who you are. It affects how you think and how you choose to communicate. To a large extent, it determines your assumptions regarding history, values, current events, politics, and religion. Your generation also affects what you expect from a career, as well as how you regard management and leadership styles.

4. How You Think About Money

Before I even start, some of you have different reactions to the word *money*. To some, it represents what they want. If they get honest with themselves, they are a whole lot more interested in having more money than finding their purpose or being authentic.

To others, money is evil; and they think they shouldn't want it… even though they do. Somewhere along the line, they were taught that money is the root of evil, and it is just greedy to want more of the stuff. Actually, the verse goes like this: "For the *love* of money is a root of all kinds of evil." While it is normal to want to have a better life, if you love money more than people or God, you have a problem.

How you think about money is a function of your assumptions and the way you were taught, your gender, and a predisposition based on your purpose. Do you assume that money is scarce, that it's all in the hands of the rich? Or do you assume there is enough money to go around for anyone who wants to earn it? Those are assumptions, but what are the facts?

> ### The number one thing Americans want is more money.
> ### —Frank Luntz

According to *What Americans Really Want, Really* by Frank Luntz, the research shows that the number one thing Americans want is more money. However, why they want it is different for men than it is for women. His research shows that men want more money to have more freedom. They also want it for more toys...so they can enjoy their freedom. It's like the adage, "He who dies with the most stuff wins."

Women also want more money. Their reasons, however, have more to do with personal security and alleviating financial fear. With the rise of fatherlessness in America and a trend where males seem to be abdicating their traditional roles as providers, more women are taking their financial security into their own hands.

Lastly, we are predisposed, or naturally wired, to think about money in one of the following ways:

◊ Security
◊ Comfort
◊ Wealth

Your predisposition to one of these ways of thinking can be heavily influenced by several factors, the major one being your personality. Let me explain.

Security

A predisposition to thinking in terms of *security* means you don't like risk. If that's you, you probably want a secure job, in an established company, that has good benefits. Safe investments that can get you the American dream in a nice neighborhood sound good to you. In addition to almost all women, security is what appeals to the largest of the four main personality types described by the DISC (the S type personality) personality assessments. Since about half the population is women and 69% of the total population has the S personality as a top trait, you can see why most people think in terms of security when it comes to money. Politicians and advertisers know this as well, and they target almost all of their marketing efforts toward those who most want security.

Comfort

People who are predisposed to think about money in terms of *comfort* are prone to taking significantly more risks. They see money as a means to increase their comfort in life. To one person money for comfort means working overtime or a second job to get a bigger TV and a nicer La-Z-Boy. To another person, it means taking a high risk (in the eyes of the person who prefers security), commission-only job so they can have a nice beach house in addition to their residence.

These are the people we would normally call "rich." They make a lot of money, and they spend a lot of money. Many of the "comfort" people also have a high D or I personality. The D-I or I-D personalities are usually outspoken, people-oriented, and driven. They make the best salespeople and often occupy CEO positions. A friend of mine in the Marine Corps used to tell me, "If you have money in the bank and vacation time on the books you aren't living right." He became a successful partner in a large brokerage firm in Manhattan. Go figure!

Wealth

People who think in terms of *wealth* exercise delayed gratification, take calculated risks, and have a plan for their money. Often a wealth-oriented person may live right next door to you, and you'd never know it until they moved into their new mansion they purchased with cash. Many people would like to be rich, but very few are oriented and plan to be wealthy. A wealthy person can come from any of the personality traits, but they probably have at least some degree of C in their personality blend. It takes planning and restraint to become wealthy, and those are C-like traits.

How you think about money is part of who you are. Even if you are predisposed to seek security, it doesn't mean you can't have comfort or wealth. It just means you think about security first. One way of thinking is not better or worse than another, but how you think about money will be a factor in your purpose. If your purpose is to make a difference for the entire planet, then you will probably need large sums of money to make that happen. If your purpose is to be an influence in your community, then the amount of money you will need may not be as large.

An authentic person recognizes their predisposition toward money and acts accordingly. A person who is not authentic may use money, credit, and debt to buy things to impress others rather than being true to their nature. Knowing whether you are more prone to security, comfort, or wealth will give you confidence in this aspect of who you are.

5. *How You Give and Receive Love*

In his book *The Five Love Languages*, Gary Chapman tells us that we don't all give or receive love the same way. When I first read his book, I was amazed. I didn't think there was anything new that I could discover about my wife or our marriage. Obviously, that wasn't true, because I learned about her personality and strengths after about 20 years of being married to her. So, discovering that we gave and received love differently shouldn't have been a surprise. But it was.

Just like your personality and the other aspects that combine to make you so unique, your way of loving is unique. Gary Chapman boils love languages down to five different types, but just as with the four major types of personalities, each person is a blend. He says that we primarily love in one of these five ways:

1. Giving and receiving gifts
2. Acts of service
3. Spending quality time
4. Physical touch
5. Words of affirmation

If someone gives you a gift, no matter how small or large the gift, and that makes you feel special and loved, then your love language may be gifts. If someone doing chores for you makes you feel especially appreciated, then acts of service may be your love language. When just being in the same room, doing nothing in particular, or being together on a road trip makes you feel special, then quality time is your love language. If holding hands, a back rub, or a head massage tells you that, no matter what else is going on, he still loves you, then physical touch may be your love language. If your heart warms when she tells you how much she appreciates you and that you are great in her eyes, then your love language may be words of affirmation.

One language is not better than another, and you may have a couple of languages that stand out for you, but one will be your dominant language. It is important to remember that just because you receive love in a certain way does not necessarily mean that the one you love receives love in the same way. That would be rare. So, not only do you need to be aware of your own language, but you need to be able to speak the language of the one you love.

I am laughing inside as I think of the mistakes I have made with Mary in this area. When we were newly married, we lived in Encinitas, California. Florists from all over the country purchased the beautiful flowers that grew on the hills in Encinitas. On any back-road around Encinitas, you could find flower stands selling beautiful bouquets of locally grown flowers at really good prices.

Being a loving husband and trying to show my new wife how much I thought of her, I would frequently stop at a flower stand and buy an arrangement then put it in a vase on our dining room table for her. Now, I should tell you I am not a flower guy, and giving or receiving gifts is not my love language. I was doing this for Mary because I had seen in movies and on TV that girls like this kind of stuff.

Several days went by and not a peep from Mary. I finally mustered the courage to bring it up to my new bride. I asked her if she liked the flowers. Her response was, "Oh my goodness, I didn't even see them. Those are nice. Thank you." That was it! So, I did a very intelligent thing. I didn't get offended but asked her if gifts or flowers did anything for her. She liked flowers, but only if she grew them in her garden. As far as gifts went, they were certainly appreciated, but she did not need them to tell her I loved her. I am a lucky man!

I discovered her love language by accident. We had an awesome Italian restaurant close to where we lived, and Friday night pizza was a ritual for me. We would often find ourselves at Papachino's restaurant in Del Mar, waiting for a table on Friday nights. Usually, Mary would be exhausted from the week's work, and she would put her legs up on my lap as we waited. One Friday I started giving her a foot massage, and I think she went to heaven. She kept saying, "Oh, that feels so good," over and over.

One of the waitresses overheard her and looked right at me. She asked, "Do you have a brother?" I guess the waitress's love language was physical touch, as was Mary's. Notice, I didn't say groping or having sex when I said physical touch. To this day, no matter how tense things might be between us, if I scratch her back or her head before we go to sleep, Mary knows I still love her and that everything is good between us.

I have a good friend who likes massages, so he has a habit of giving people shoulder massages as a form of greeting. Many people like it, but I am not one of them. I finally had to tell him I loved him like a brother, but if he ever tried to give me another shoulder massage, I was going to break his hands. Physical touch is NOT my love language. For me to give love in this way to my wife is an effort, but I know how much it means to her, so I am happy to give her love in the form she needs.

Even though I sort of knew her love language after years of being together, it wasn't confirmed until we read *The Five Love Languages*. Mary wasn't sure of my language until she read the book and we had a chance to discuss it together. I'm one of those people who likes order, and I am visually oriented. Seeing things out of place in our home, or seeing our home become dirty, really bothers me. Mary often doesn't even notice the things that bug me. Remember, she didn't see the flowers either.

So, to keep a sense of order in our home, I started picking up and doing a lot of the cleaning in our house.

She told me she thought I was doing this as an act of service for her, which is not her love language, nor mine. I finally had to set her straight. I wasn't doing those things for her; I was doing them for me. If she did them, I would appreciate it; but I just liked the sense of order, not the idea that she was doing something for me. What I love is just spending time together. Whether watching a movie together on the couch, riding bikes, or exploring someplace new, just knowing she wants to be with me is what makes me feel loved.

It is sad, but we have all heard the stories of couples who have been married for a long time and then divorce. Sometimes, they hang on until their children leave the nest, or sometimes they are in their sixties and just can't stay together any longer. There is a story in *The Five Love Languages* about a couple like this. The man reached the end of his rope but agreed to get some marriage counseling before they called it quits. In counseling, he said that he just couldn't please her. He did this for her, and he did that for her, and she never appreciated him for it. Obviously, his love language was acts of service.

His wife, on the other hand, told him that all she ever wanted was to spend time with him. Sitting on the couch together or watching TV or a movie would have meant the world to her, but he was always too busy fixing the cars or doing this or that. This couple had been together for over 40 years, yet neither of them knew what they needed to do to feel mutual love.

How do you give and receive love? Don't you think it would be a good idea to know this about yourself? Fortunately, several tools can aid you in figuring it out. In the Resources section, you will find a link to the *Five Love Languages Quiz*. If you are married or are thinking of being married, I would recommend you have the other person in your relationship take the quiz also. It should be revealing, and it could save you a lot of heartaches.

There is another aspect of giving love that is important. As I have already mentioned, my personality profile has described me as being cold, critical, and aloof—not exactly words that I would regard as being praiseworthy, nor are they very loving. It took me a while to accept that those words were pretty accurate.

I wanted, and prayed for, help in becoming more loving and compassionate towards people. The problem was I was not wired that way, and being loving and compassionate took real effort and felt unnatural for me. Then I discovered something that resolved my dilemma. Until I got okay with who I really was, there was no way I would discover my GIFT.

Once I discovered my GIFT and then began to develop it and give it away, I learned how I was meant to be compassionate and loving. Now, in the process of using my GIFT, my compassion, patience, and love flow without effort. The more I use my GIFT, the more these virtues become evident. So, if you are having a difficult time being the loving person you want to be, my advice would be to first accept who you are—then discover your GIFT.

6. GIFT

In a word, your GIFT is what makes you *unique*. Your GIFT is a single talent you can develop to greatness as manifested in your unique way of thinking.

> ### *Your GIFT is a single talent you can develop to greatness as manifested in your unique way of thinking.*

No two minds think the same way. Your way of thinking is by design and for a reason. It was specifically created for you. So, you are not weird…you are GIFTed.

The talent I am speaking of is not the physical part of talent, but the mental part of your talent. For instance, an athlete may have superior physical attributes, but only when those attributes are married with passion and creative thinking (both of which will be addressed later) would we say he or she is GIFTed.

There is something that you think about better than anyone else. We may observe it as "talent," but it is much more than that. It is your special GIFT.

Your GIFT is the way God designed you to succeed in life—how He created you to make a difference is by operating in your GIFT. If you have ever heard someone talk about a time when they were in "their zone," they were probably talking about operating in their GIFT. People can't rock your boat, and usually don't even try, when you operate in your GIFT because you are supremely confident about what you are doing. That special and unique way of thinking is what you were given to succeed in life.

Your GIFT is the way you were designed to show love. Employing your GIFT is a joy, it makes you feel at peace, and it gives you exceptional patience with people. Operating in your GIFT benefits others in a way that can only be called love. If you have ever struggled with the impossibility of loving others as yourself it is because you were trying to make yourself do something you thought was right. When you give your GIFT, loving others happens naturally, almost without effort.

Why don't people know they have a special GIFT?

Finding out who you are can be kind of fun, especially if you do it in a group. But for some reason, the idea of having a GIFT and employing it for your purpose intimidates many people. Very few people ever seek their GIFT, and some go out of their way to avoid it.

Employing your GIFT is the epitome of being authentic. So, if you want to be authentic and reap all its benefits, you'll need to find your GIFT first.

The First Step in Finding Your GIFT

The first step in finding your GIFT is overcoming inertia.

Inertia is a tendency to do nothing or to remain unchanged. It can also be defined as the property by which something continues in its existing state of rest or uniform motion in a straight line unless that state is changed by an external force.

This is a fancy way of saying that it takes effort to change.

Whether you are doing nothing at all or you're going at warp speed in the wrong direction, something has to break you free of the inertia that's keeping you stuck where you are.

Just the fact that you are already reading this means you are in the process of overcoming inertia.

You have a seed of greatness in you. Notice that was a statement, not a question. It is a fact that you have a GIFT. When your GIFT is developed, you will find that some people will call you a genius. But don't get too stuck on yourself…everyone has a GIFT.

If you knew you had a GIFT, and it could take you as far as you wanted to go in life, wouldn't you want to know what it is? Yet the fear of discovering just how great you are can be overwhelming to many. It is much easier to go through life without knowing how great you can be. Then no one will expect anything of you, including yourself. Ultimately, I guess you could call this the fear of success.

The word *greatness* throws some people. As soon as you tell them they could be great at something, their negative self-talk kicks in telling them they could never be great at anything. They feel inadequate because either they failed at something or someone told them they were inadequate—a loser.

Almost everyone feels inadequate somehow. Don't you? I have had many more people tell me what I couldn't do than what I could do. I once had a dream to be a professional baseball pitcher. The problem was my fastball wasn't all that fast, and sometimes my curveball didn't curve. I felt inadequate, and no one argued with me.

Some people don't try to be great at anything because they have a messed-up view of what it means to be humble or meek. They think you can't be both great and humble at the same time. Your *acting* meek doesn't serve the world; *being* meek does. Meekness lies in knowing your GIFT was given to you by your Creator and that you did nothing to deserve it. Your GIFT is not about you. It is about making a difference.

When I ask people what they want to do, almost all of them tell me they don't know. What they do know is that they want to make a difference somehow. They want to know they have something they can contribute. They want to know they are valued, and they want to be appreciated. Isn't that how you feel?

The problem is that you can't pretend to be small and still be significant at the same time. If you have something in you that is brilliant and for which you are recognized as being great, then having a false sense of humility so you won't stick out in a crowd doesn't help anything. Real humility is using your GIFT to its fullest potential so the maximum number of people can benefit from it. You won't need to seek recognition because you will naturally be recognized for your GIFT. If you still feel the need to seek recognition, then you are probably not operating in a God-given GIFT.

> *Real humility is using your GIFT to its fullest potential so the maximum number of people can benefit from it.*

Have you ever held back your talent so that you didn't overshadow someone else? If so, why did you do it? Was it to make the other person feel better? If so, how many people benefited from your holding back? How many more would have been blessed if you had let your light shine instead?

I think all of us can relate to the feeling of holding back to not upset the apple cart at some time or other. The question is why? Sometimes it is because we are not confident in our GIFT. Sometimes we are afraid of offending people if we overshadow them. Sometimes this fear is so great we don't even look for what we do well or seek the GIFT we have been blessed with.

So, what's the point? The point is that our biggest fear is not that we are inadequate. Our biggest fear is that we have something awesome inside us and that it may overwhelm us and take us somewhere we may think we do not want to go. That fear is the biggest reason people stay stuck where they are and pretend to be someone less than who they really are.

Faith that you have a GIFT and faith that you have an awesome purpose can overcome the fear of being inadequate. When you discover your GIFT, you'll see that any fear you may have will start to fade, and hope will start to take its place—hope that you really can make a difference. It is said that faith comes by hearing, so let me tell you one more time: you have a GIFT, and it is perfect for you.

Skills vs. Talents

Now the BIG question: How do you find this God-given talent—your GIFT? Aren't you wondering this? You already have the first piece of the answer—your personality. Remember, your personality is another God-given gift. He predisposed you to behave in a certain way, on purpose. In other words, knowing your personality (how you naturally behave) is not just a fun exercise. Knowing your personality is a major part of discovering who you are and what you are supposed to do with your life.

Likewise, knowing your GIFT is a major part of discovering who you are and what you are supposed to do with your life. In fact, you could say it is the missing key to your Authenticity Advantage.

Before I jump in to explaining your GIFT, let me make a distinction between skills and talents. As I've already stated, your GIFT is a single talent you can develop to greatness as manifested in your unique way of thinking. Many use the terms skill and talent interchangeably, but that is a mistake.

There is a preoccupation with skills in the workplace today. A skill is something you are accomplished at as the result of hard work and effort. You can develop a skill for which you have no talent, but it will always require much more effort and concentration.

Early in my flight training in Pensacola, Florida, I had a revealing experience about developing my skill as a pilot. I was a new lieutenant, and my instructor that day was a Marine captain. The graded part of the flight was over, and the captain was flying the airplane back to base. There was a lot of turbulence from the thunderstorms that surrounded us, and I took a moment to watch the lightning strike the ground. The captain saw me looking out the canopy and gave me this stern instruction; "Lieutenant Gilroy, you could be a good pilot if you kept your head in the cockpit!" That was the day I realized that developing skills was hard work and not much fun.

As a Marine Corps pilot, I worked hard to be skilled, probably because I vividly remembered that rebuke. No matter how far I progressed in my training, it was always hard work for me. I would come back from missions drenched in sweat and completely exhausted. Some of my friends who were "talented" pilots came back from the same missions exhilarated and ready to do it again. It was natural for them, but not for me.

Talent comes naturally and with little effort. You do not have to think about using your talent, it just flows out of you. You may have several talents, but only one of them can be developed to greatness.

Everyone has a talent. It is not just athletes, musicians, and entertainers that have talent, as some of the popular television shows would have you believe. Your talent is how you express the unique way in which you think. You may have a talent for organization or systems, or you may have a talent that enables you to intuitively know what others feel. No amount of learning can rival a natural talent.

To achieve greatness, your talent needs to be developed. That means that using your talent requires effort, but it is not the kind of effort you would consider to be a struggle or drudgery. The passion to develop your talent comes with the talent because you will naturally desire to use it.

Using your Authenticity Advantage should not be exhausting but exhilarating. That's because your Authenticity Advantage incorporates your GIFT (your single talent that can be developed to greatness) and not skills.

What Is Your GIFT?

So, what is the unique talent at which you are the best, the one you are supposed to develop to greatness that comes from the unique way you think? You could be one of the remarkably few who intuitively has known your GIFT from birth or you could have a divine revelation where God shows you; but, for most of us, we must find it for ourselves. Fortunately, the Gallup organization has an assessment that does just that. Their assessment is the result of a forty-year study of human talents in which they surveyed more than 10 million people worldwide and identified 34 different talents that a person could possess.

CliftonStrengths Assessment by Gallup is referenced for you in the Resources section. It is a tool that will accurately identify and order your 34 talents from greatest to least, and it is the best indicator of how you think available today.

The reason I recommend this assessment is because it proves something you probably already know intuitively: you are a one-of-a-kind, unique creation. The chances that someone else has the same top five talents as you, and in the same order, is one in 33 million. At first, I thought that was a huge number that proved just how unique your thinking is. But since the US has a population of about 331 million, that means there are potentially 10 people in the United States who think just like you. Today's world population is about 7.875 billion, which means there are possibly 238 people in the world who think like you. So, maybe you aren't so unique. But wait, there's more.

The odds that someone has all 34 of your talents in the same order is one in 259,000,000,000,000,000,000,000,000,000,000,000,000! That makes it statistically impossible for someone to think exactly like you do.

Most people are either unaware of their talents or are unable to describe them. They have no idea how unique their talent is, or its value. How important do you think it would be to find out the top God-given talent you possess—your GIFT? And yet far too many people go an entire lifetime with their GIFT still undiscovered.

There is a short story from Samuel Clemens that describes why finding your GIFT is so important to making a difference. It goes like this:

> *A man died and met Saint Peter at the Pearly Gates.*
> *He said, "Saint Peter, I have been interested in*
> *military history for many years. Who was the greatest*
> *general of all time?"*
>
> *Saint Peter quickly responded, "Oh that's a simple*
> *question. It's that man right over there."*
>
> *"You must be mistaken," responded the man, now*

very perplexed. "I knew that man on earth, and he was just a common laborer."

"That's right, my friend," assured Saint Peter. "He would have been the greatest general of all time if he had been a general."

Understanding Your GIFT

Just as with my personality assessment, I was surprised at how accurate CliftonStrengths Assessment was at finding and describing my talents. I found that one's GIFT (the top talent in your assessment) lines up perfectly with your personality. Without the right personality, your GIFT could not be used effectively. This is because your personality is a function of behavior, while your GIFT describes your unique way of thinking.

The talent assessment from CliftonStrengths is a bit more complicated than the DISC personality assessment. That's because it identifies 34 different talents with millions of potential combinations to describe you, whereas the DISC personality assessment is based on a combination of just four choices. You can choose to receive a report of just your top five strengths or all 34. I recommend you choose the Top 5 CliftonStrengths report in order to keep things simple.

Understanding the assessment is not difficult, but it requires a bit more explanation if you really want to get something out of it. You will be amazed at how much your GIFT (your top talent in the assessment) is a natural part of who you are.

The top talent in my assessment is Maximizer. A Maximizer thinks differently from the 33 other talents listed in the assessment. People with a Maximizer GIFT focus on personal and group excellence. They notice the unique traits that differentiate each individual and Maximizers seek to transform something strong into something superb.

Your top talent will be equally unique, especially as you combine it with your other talents. I found the assessment extremely useful because not only did it identify my top talents, but it also gave me ideas for how to use my unique way of thinking. The top talent identified in the assessment is what I call your GIFT. It is the predominant way you are wired to think. Ordering the other 33 talents helps to further explain how you think and how different you are from others. Again, the chances that someone else has the same order of talents as you are virtually zero.

How Your GIFT Fits on a Team

Your GIFT is meant to work in harmony with people who have other GIFTs. That way no one must be all things to all people. Ideally, you should work with people who have talents that you don't have. That allows you to continue to develop your GIFT and not be stuck in the unproductive pursuit of improving your weaknesses.

As you employ your GIFT and take advantage of your authenticity, it is good to keep this in mind and to remember that no man (or woman) is an island. Your GIFT is needed, not just for your benefit, but for others as well. When you develop your GIFT to its full potential, you become a part of something greater than yourself that makes a difference.

Every person whom the world views as great had one thing in common: They were focused on what they did exceptionally well.

Ralph Waldo Emerson called it finding *"your best self."*

Napoleon Hill called it a *"definite major purpose."*

Saint Paul called it the *"one thing I do."*

Regardless of what you choose to call it, your GIFT unlocks the door to your Authenticity Advantage. However, to receive the greatest benefit of your GIFT, it must be used in combination with the GIFTs of others.

You Are Chosen

You do not choose your GIFT. It was chosen for you and given to you from your birth. This way of thinking can rub us Americans the wrong way, so let me explain.

> ## *You don't choose your GIFT. It was chosen for you and given to you from your birth.*

If you were raised in the United States, you might have been brought up to believe in self-determination and that you are the captain of your fate. To some degree, that is true. You do have the ability to choose, and you can say "no" to things you don't want to do. Our Declaration of Independence states that we have been "endowed by (our) Creator with certain unalienable Rights, that among these are Life, Liberty and the pursuit of Happiness." As a republic, we have more liberty to choose our destinies than most countries.

Even so, to say you can do anything that you put your mind to is not entirely correct. As Tom Rath says in *StrengthsFinder 2.0:*

> *A revision to the 'You-can-be-anything-you-want-to-be' maxim might be more accurate: You cannot be anything you want to be—but you can be more of who you already are.*

You must work within the talents and attributes you possess. If you are five feet tall, have no vertical jump, and can't shoot, your chances of being an NBA superstar are remote, no matter how much you want it. Your physical size, your personality, and your talent are gifts you were born with. Your choice involves using them and developing them. You cannot choose to be six feet tall if your mature height is five feet. Likewise, you cannot be a great singer if you were born tone-deaf. In the United States, you have the liberty to pursue goals and dreams, even if you have no gifts in those areas...but that does not mean you will be successful.

My point is this: you are who you are, and you have a very special GIFT for a reason. The sooner you accept your GIFT and who you really are rather than wishing for talents and attributes that are not yours, the sooner you will discover your purpose. The sooner you develop your GIFT, that one talent you do best, the sooner you will fulfill your purpose and receive the prize that was set aside just for you. Don't be like the man in Mark Twain's story, accepting life as a common laborer when he was born to be the greatest general.

Putting It All Together

The six aspects of who you really are fit together to give you a more complete picture than any one of them do by themselves. That is certainly true of how personality and GIFT work together.

The above chart is a representation of my personality profile. A C-D personality is a natural problem solver. My personality assessment says a C-D personality has the "ability to identify potential problems and detect errors. He can bring logic and understanding while providing logical steps to evaluate and analyze information. He excels at developing a strategy and methods to solve problems. "

How have the people I have worked for tried to leverage my personality? I'm the guy employers would send in to find out what was wrong and fix it. During my first overseas deployment in the Marine Corps, my squadron had a helicopter crash because of a problem with the fuel system. The commanding officer chose me to identify the problem and recommend changes to prevent it from happening again.

At my next duty station in Washington, DC, my unit had some issues with their budget. With no experience or training in finance or budgets, my new commanding officer chose me to find the issues and fix them. So, a trend was beginning to emerge of my bosses intuitively knowing my personality and putting me into a position to fix problems. So far, so good.

But then…when I mistakenly chose a career in sales, guess what I did? I tried to fix sales approaches or strategies, find or develop better products, and solve problems my customers were having. Since many businesses are very short-term focused, rarely looking beyond the next couple of months, my bosses wanted me to put my efforts toward immediate returns. They realized I could help them find problems, but they wanted short-term solutions with immediate results.

My Maximizer GIFT paints a different picture. It acknowledges that I have problem-solving abilities, but it says I would not be using my GIFT if I chase short-term results. It also says to focus on long-term relationships instead of trying to fix what is broken. I should look for what is good and try to make it superb. Instead of focusing on sales, I should look for ways to help people.

For the first several years after I left the Marines, I did not know what my GIFT was. I was between jobs when I discovered the CliftonStrengths Assessment and began to understand myself better. That's when I received a call from a recruiter. He had my resume and asked me if I knew anything about night vision devices, which I did. Then he started talking about a position selling night vision goggles to the military. He had my interest until he said the job was in Allentown, Pennsylvania. All I could think of was a Billy Joel song about miners in Allentown, so I said, "No way!" That's when he told me the last guy who had the position made $500,000. I quickly revised my statement to, "Tell me more about Allentown."

The recruiter asked me to send him my last two evaluations from the military to go along with my resume. So, after finding those evaluations, I thought it might be a good idea to read them first. I was amazed. In the narrative section of both evaluations, my commanders had perfectly described the talents as revealed on my CliftonStrengths assessment. Now I should interject that not all commanding officers are that good at knowing their subordinates, but these two lieutenant colonels were exceptional; and one of them went on to become a major general.

My point is that I originally took their comments the wrong way. I thought they were just making up flattering stuff to make me look good for promotion. It never dawned on me to ask them to explain why they wrote those comments. If I had, it would have saved me an enormous amount of time and frustration, and it certainly would have led me to better career choices. I would have learned to not only use my personality, but my GIFT as well.

With these stories in mind, do you see that you can be operating in your personality, at least to some degree, and yet not be using your GIFT? When that happens, you'll find your work exhausting.

However, when you use your GIFT in your work, you will find it exhilarating and fulfilling.

When you consider your personality, your gender, how you think about money, how you give and receive love, and your generation, they all have an effect on how you think. They all affect your GIFT. Without understanding how these six aspects work together it is nearly impossible to know what you want.

Chapter 6
Desire and Passion

We often use words in our everyday language without really knowing what they mean. This is especially true with the words desire and passion.

I have had the privilege to associate with some senior law enforcement officers at training meetings all over the country. After a few discussions about leadership, it dawned on me that most of these guys did not agree with each other. They all seemed to have a different take on the subject, and there was no common concept of what leadership was.

I wondered why. So, I asked a few of the senior law enforcement professionals if they could tell me what they thought leadership was. None of them had the same definition. This meant that all their conversations and training were starting from different foundations. It also meant that as they trained their own departments, the people being trained also heard something different, depending on their preconceptions of leadership.

Setting a common foundation based on a precise definition of words is critical to being able to communicate concepts to others. While starting a leadership discussion with an appropriate definition is important, it is even more critical when discussing your desire.

I used to associate the words desire and passion with lust and greed because of things I heard in church when I was young. My assumption was that desire and passion were bad and to be avoided. What are your assumptions and how would you interpret these words? I had to "unlearn" what I thought I knew and find out what these words really meant.

It is very important that you understand exactly what I want to convey as we go forward, so forgive me for being so boring as to use some definitions.

Desire means to long for or hope for something that you expect to receive. Knowing who you are and knowing your GIFT activates your hope because you know it is possible. You may not expect to get what you wish or dream for, but you do expect to get what you desire.

Passion is a strong, active, intense, emotional desire that enables you to endure hardship, even suffering. Passion gives you the endurance to stay the course and overcome the obstacles that will get in the way of you obtaining the desire of your heart.

Desire Is the Starting Point

There is a proverb that says: "Hope deferred makes the heart sick, but desire fulfilled is a tree of life."

The main reason that so many people have sick hearts is that they don't expect to get what they desire—they don't have hope. Hope can be defined as having a positive expectation of something good. And the reason they don't have hope is that they don't know their identity.

A sick heart can cause heart disease and high blood pressure. It can be one of the reasons so many take antidepressant medication by buckets full and many are suicidal. Even those that aren't depressed are often angry or fearful. There doesn't seem to be a lot of joy in the world.

The same proverb that speaks about sick hearts also has the solution. It says that "desire fulfilled is a tree of life." This means that fulfilling your desire brings a long, happy, joyful, and abundant life.

So, what do you want—a sick heart or a tree of life? Your choice has to do with your desire.

In his famous book, *Think and Grow Rich,* Napoleon Hill says:

> *Desire is the starting point of all achievement.*

In his book *Law of Success,* Hill says:

> *Desire is the factor which determines what your definite purpose in life shall be.*

But nowhere in his writings does he tell you how to find your desire.

When you know who you are and you know your GIFT, you will naturally want to use your GIFT. Wanting to use your GIFT is the desire of your heart. The problem is that most people don't know who they are nor their GIFT.

How Do You Find Your Desire?

I'm not a GIFTed conversationalist. I do, however, love to talk to people about their purpose. I've never heard anyone start a conversation about purpose on their own; it just doesn't happen. Suppose I walked up to a stranger and just asked, "Hey there Billy Bob, you don't know me, but can you tell me your purpose?" What kind of reaction do you think I would get? So, I had to come up with a way to get people talking about purpose.

The way I introduce the idea of purpose to people is to ask them what they do. Most people don't think that is too threatening a question. I then follow up with, "What do you *really* want to do?" Since at least 70% of employees are not engaged while at work according to the Gallup organization, I know that most of the people I ask will tell me they are not doing what they want.

If someone asked you that question, how would you answer? Most of the time what people will say is that they don't know, but they wish they could figure it out. It's not an easy question to answer.

What you want is another way of saying *desire*. Since most people don't know what they want, if you push them for an answer, they will tell you the kind of possessions they want or the kind of vacation they would like to take, or they'll tell you they'd like to retire. Those are all learned responses as the result of marketing and advertising; you have been influenced to say that you want those things.

Once you know who you are and your GIFT, you will know your desire. You will desire to use your GIFT. If your GIFT is Maximizing, then you won't be happy unless you are maximizing something. If your GIFT is Activating (another of the 34 strengths from the CliftonStrengths assessment), you will want to activate something or tell someone what to do (hopefully not your spouse). If your GIFT is Learning (yet another strength), you won't be able to sit around doing nothing, you will have to find something to learn.

Knowing your identity is liberating because you can fulfill your desire. Until you experience the thrill of beginning to fulfill your desire, you haven't lived. That's why it is a common saying that most people go to the grave with their songs still in them. I want you to sing your song. We all want to hear it.

Passion

Have you ever met someone truly passionate about what they did? How did you feel when you were around them? I'll bet you weren't lukewarm. Passionate people either attract others or repel them. There is usually no middle ground. Even if you are repelled by a passionate person, you might wish you had that same kind of emotion for something in your life.

It is passion that drives people over, under, around, or through obstacles in their way. They intensely desire something, they know they have the GIFT to make it happen, and they are confident in the outcome. They keep going when passionless people would stop. To others, the person with passion appears to be superhuman.

However, if you take a close look at passionate people, there may be nothing about them that is superhuman. That is because desire and passion are spiritual assets. You can't see them, touch them, smell them, hear them, or taste them. But you know they are there.

Passion builds businesses, writes songs, paints masterpieces, attracts people, and lifts their spirits. Passion is the mother of invention. It helps you to endure and persist until you get what you desire. It also involves a strong emotion that is contagious and moving. We all want to be around passionate people.

Until I found my GIFT, I felt as if God had left the "passion chip" out of my design. I couldn't get passionate about anything even though I had been looking for something to put 100% of myself into since childhood. It seemed I was okay at most of the things I tried, from sports to music to schoolwork, but nothing made me want to go all in.

To make things worse, my less than 100% effort was still better than most of my competition, so I was drifting through life "appearing" to be successful. The problem was that it wasn't good enough for me. I have found that "good enough" keeps a lot of people from living with passion. It is just comfortable enough to keep them from finding their GIFT. This is where good becomes the enemy of great.

> *"Good enough" keeps people from living with passion. It is just comfortable enough to keep them from finding their GIFT.*

I am fortunate to have cultivated a relationship with a very successful and passionate business leader and mentor, named Jack. What's interesting is that my dad's name was also Jack, and he too was very passionate. Jack (my mentor) is focused and extremely self-disciplined, so much so that he can be intimidating if you don't know him. To me, his self-discipline appeared to take enormous effort and willpower, and to be honest I didn't know if I had that in me. Consequently, I wondered if I could ever be as passionate as him.

I give my mentor credit for three impactful revelations in my life: introducing me to the Holy Spirit, teaching me how to think for myself, and acquainting me with the success principles of Napoleon Hill. To be clear, I don't agree with everything Hill wrote, but he was closer to the mark on success than anyone else has been to this day.

In *How to Raise Your Own Salary,* an obscure book written by Hill, he has a back-and-forth conversation with Andrew Carnegie. Andrew Carnegie was the founder of the US Steel Corporation and the richest person in the world at the time. At one point Carnegie said to Hill:

> *Obsessional desires make self-discipline very easy. It is no trouble at all to form thought-habits if one has a definite motive, backed by a strong emotional desire for the attainment of the object of the motive.*

In two sentences, Hill described why I could not seem to get passionate about anything and why self-discipline looked like such an overwhelming chore. I didn't know my desire. Again, your desire is to employ your GIFT. I have found that when you find your GIFT and discover your desires you will realize two things: first, they have always been there; and second, passion always accompanies them.

> *Wanting to use your GIFT is the desire of your heart, and passion will always accompany it.*

Before I discovered this, I once asked Jack how I could find passion. I swear he looked at me like I was from Mars. The idea that someone didn't know their desire or wasn't passionate was foreign to him. Apparently, it was to Hill also because he doesn't tell you how to find your desire. In fact, no passionate person could tell me how to get what they had.

I don't know about you, but that was a huge missing link for me. Can you imagine what the world would be like if even a fraction of the population knew their GIFT and were passionate about giving it? Think of the problems that would disappear overnight!

That's why finding your desire and living with passion is such a big deal. It really makes a difference!

Some Clues About Passion

Before I discovered my GIFT, even though I didn't know how to find my desire, there were moments when I was passionate. Those moments are clues. I remember attending a seminar in which the very passionate speaker said he woke up irritated every morning. I leaned over to my wife and whispered, "I can relate," to which she just shook her head in irritation and said, "I know you can." It was funny how a revelation to me was obvious to her. That's also a clue.

What the speaker made clear to me was that his daily, irritated attitude was just part of his personality. It wasn't negative. It was how he was wired. That is exactly how I felt, but someone else had to express it before I realized the truth of the matter. Now, I needed to figure out why I was irritated and what caused it?

Some people become emotional more easily than others, so finding their passion may be a little bit easier. But I don't get overly excited either positively or negatively, so the emotion I have is most often expressed as irritation. This is important because a key component of passion is a strong emotion. You will need to recognize how you express emotion to find your passion.

For you, finding your passion could be expressed through emotions of anger or agitation. It could be something that deeply disturbs you because no one is doing anything about it. It could be something that seems like an injustice or a crime to you or something that disturbs your sense of decency.

On the other hand, what you are passionate about could be something that warms your heart or makes you feel compassionate or loving. If you find yourself asking why someone isn't doing something regarding what you feel emotional about, that's also a clue. You are probably the one who is supposed to do that "something." In fact, you are probably uniquely suited to do that "something" because you have the personality and GIFT to make it happen.

This all became clear to me while walking through a shopping mall one day. I saw a group of eighteen to twenty-year-olds hanging out together, which wasn't unusual at all. They weren't acting up or unruly, but what caught my attention was the way they were dressed. They were all dressed in black and were heavily tattooed, with more metal in their faces than a hardware store. My irritation at the sight quickly turned to anger, which isn't usual for me.

I didn't know why I felt that way, so I made myself do something very uncharacteristic. I went up and talked to them. At first, I noticed their eyes were dead, like nothing was going on inside, but as I started to talk to them, I found they were nice kids. That's not what I expected.

I expected these Goths, as I later found out they were called, to be belligerent. That was not the case at all. I think they were grateful to speak to an adult in a normal conversation. What I found was that they were lost and had no idea of their potential. While most of the people I talked with wanted to make a difference, these kids didn't. They had given up on the world and didn't expect to amount to anything. That made me want to find their parents and smack them.

Here's what that trip to the mall showed me: The sight of those young people dressed in black got my attention and made me feel irritated. The irritation grew to an intense emotion when I spoke to them. All of this centered on how lost they were and that, unless something dramatically changed, these kids would have a wasted life. They had no clue how awesome they were or that they each had a GIFT; certainly, none of them seemed to be looking for it. That bothered me. That's probably because I wasn't living up to my own potential either.

What's funny is that the Goths didn't bother my wife a bit. That's another clue. If something makes you emotional but doesn't affect others as much as you, then you are probably the one that's supposed to do something about it. Mary is a health fanatic, and she has been able to teach people to lose a substantial amount of weight and feel significantly better. When she sees an overweight person or a woman with hormone issues, it greatly bothers her. Me, not so much.

Maybe you are one of those that gets irritated too, and your spouse or best friend doesn't understand why. What is it that gets you upset? (I don't mean people cutting you off in traffic, that ticks off everybody.) If you dig below the surface of the irritation, what is the underlying cause? You might have to get a little introspective, and it might be something that bothers you about yourself, but I'll bet you have a GIFT that could make a serious impact on that issue.

Confusion

Part of the reason that many people don't identify their desires and they don't live with passion is that they use the wrong words. I have heard people use words like goals, enthusiasm, motivation, self-discipline, desire, and passion interchangeably as if they all mean the same thing. That's confusing, and it's not correct.

When we try to succeed without desire and passion (which is most often the case), our only option becomes trying to *fail* our way to success. Many success books talk about how important failure is in becoming successful. To fail your way to success you need self-discipline, enthusiasm, motivation, goals, or to try to be a superhero.

The problem is that:

◊ Self-discipline is too much effort to put forth forever.

◊ Enthusiasm always fades.

◊ Motivation stops when the motivator is gone.

◊ Goals are poor substitutes for passion.

◊ Most of us aren't superheroes.

Self-discipline, enthusiasm, motivation, and goals are exerted from the outside. Either you or someone else *makes* you do something. On the other hand, desire and passion come from within. They are already there, trying to come out!

If you are told you *have* to do something that will require discipline and you *must* hit certain goals, doesn't it sound like it is going to be difficult? If you are told you will need to go to training seminars to keep motivated, doesn't that tell you that what you will be doing won't be much fun? Yet, this is what a lot of us expect. We expect it to be hard, no fun, not exciting, and probably not too fulfilling. Without passion, the only way we can endure is by an outside force.

On the other hand, if you are going to do something you desire and are passionate about, doesn't that sound like it would be exciting? If you put in long hours in pursuit of your desire, but it is something that gives you a lot of satisfaction, doesn't that beat a job where you watch the clock waiting to go home?

What if you woke up every day excited to get back to doing the thing you love, with people who energize you? When this is your way of life, you may still have goals, but now they are a way of measuring where you are with respect to where you want to be.

Enthusiasm can come and go, while passion lasts. Enthusiasm is a feeling or emotion that can be manufactured at will, and it can result in action; but that action is usually short-lived. Because enthusiasm can be created, it can also be manipulated, either by yourself or by someone charismatic enough to garner your enthusiasm. If enthusiasm is created but does not spring from passion, it will not get you the desire of your heart. It is interesting to note that other people will also be able to tell if your enthusiasm is manufactured and does not come from passion.

In the movie *Master and Commander*, Russell Crowe plays the captain of an English warship during the Napoleonic Wars. A scene in the movie shows officers of the ship having dinner in the wardroom. Crowe's character, Captain Aubrey, is asked if he will share an anecdote about Lord Admiral Nelson, a hero of the English Navy. Captain Aubrey says he has spoken with Nelson twice. "The second time he told me a story about how someone offered him a boat cloak on a cold night. He said, no, he didn't need it. He was quite warm. His zeal for king and country kept him warm." As Aubrey looks around the dining table, he notices the look of disbelief on the face of his friend, the ship's doctor. He continues, "I know it sounds absurd, and were it from another man, you would cry out, 'Oh, what pitiful stuff' and dismiss it as mere enthusiasm...but with Nelson, you felt your heart glow."

In this scene, Captain Aubrey makes the point that there is a difference between mere enthusiasm and genuine passion. The difference is huge. The heart-glowing passion to do something great is what we all hope for. This is the kind of passion that drives one forward in the face of overwhelming odds. This is the kind of passion that seems obsessive to others. It does not know the word defeat. It is the kind of passion that allows one to go the extra mile, or even the extra 10 miles, and do it with confidence and vigor. It is this kind of passion for a purpose that is the key to all great success.

People with this kind of passion exude confidence. They have a contagious optimism that stirs men's hearts. That is what Admiral Nelson described on that cold night. That's why we go to movies, to see passion in heroes (action movies), in romance (chick flicks), and in everyday lives (dramas).

Motivation is what we need to keep moving. Business leaders and sales managers will often go to great expense to orchestrate motivational events for their teams. They bring in motivational speakers to present emotional talks designed to "pump up" their staffs. They try to motivate them to get them back out on the trail, and to help them "keep on keeping on." These motivational events are designed to make sure they hit the next goal.

As we were preparing to leave the military and venture into the business world, my wife was introduced to the Amway business. Being a strong-willed leader of her own, she was quickly ushered in front of some of the top leadership in the organization to entice her to join their team. The way I found out that "we" were in "the business" was during a long-distance call while I was on my last six-month military deployment in the Philippines. It was further explained when I arrived home. Being the intelligent man that I am, I went along with Mary's business ambitions to have a pleasant homecoming (you can read between the lines).

A couple of weeks after my homecoming, and after a two-day road trip, I found myself at a huge Amway conference in Spokane, Washington. I can tell you I wasn't really happy about using my military leave for a business meeting with a bunch of strangers, especially after having been deployed overseas for six months. All that changed once I got there. The meeting was electrifying, and I wondered where these people had been all my life. They were speaking my language, and I was excited to get "our" business started.

Well, that enthusiasm lasted just about three months...just in time for the next big conference. Sure enough, I got all pumped up again, ready to tackle the world. And so, the cycle continued. The idea was to keep you motivated enough to keep working for three months to get some success under your belt.

To be honest, it worked for a while. However, I found myself relying on someone else to motivate me to build my own business instead of using my GIFT. What I found was that motivation is temporary, whereas passion endures.

> *Motivation is temporary,*
> *whereas passion endures.*

Please do not hear what I am not saying. I am not saying that motivation, enthusiasm, or goals are bad things. What I am saying is that having enthusiasm, being motivated, or reaching for goals without desire and passion will only give you very temporary results. If you are passionate about your desire, you won't need anyone to pump you up. If you are truly passionate about what you are doing, you will naturally be enthusiastic, and everyone around you will know it.

If someone must set goals for you, and then they have to manage you to make sure you hit them, it is a sure sign you are not passionate about what you are doing. All the books and management theories about goal setting were written to make people do things for which they do not have a desire or passion. Those books and management theories were probably written by people who have what DISC calls "high D" personalities. High D personalities can make themselves do things they don't want to do by giving themselves a swift (mental) kick in their rear ends. If you are not a high D personality, and you could hear the self-talk of one of these dominant, directing doers, it would probably scare you to death.

But even the D personalities can't force themselves to hit goals forever. They burn out, too. They only appear to be successful without knowing their desires. Anyone that does not know what they desire in life will have a heart with a huge hole. Anyone who is driven by something other than passion, as D personalities often are, can make a lot of people unhappy. That is because without purpose and passion abuse is inevitable.

Passion feeds causes, fuels vision, builds businesses, rights injustices, creates beauty, and is the source of compassion. Without passion, people just go through the motions and try to survive. Without passion, a normal response to a challenge is, "whatever." I hate that reply. It is dead, unemotional, uncaring, without thought, and apathetic. That is no way to go through life.

People clearly want to find what they are passionate about and can devote their lives to. But they want to be authentic in the process.

You will naturally desire to use your GIFT, and passion comes with it. It is all part of who you really are. It is your Authenticity Advantage.

Chapter 7
What Does It Mean to Think?

People have been trying to answer that question for many years. As a result, different assessments have been created to determine just how to describe your thinking. Personality assessments have been created to explain how your thinking affects behavior. Talent assessments have been developed to explain how your natural talents affect your thinking. Dr. Caroline Leaf developed an assessment called the Seven Pillars of Thought to describe how thoughts are formed in your mind. Gary Chapman developed an assessment to determine how your thoughts regarding love are expressed. And there are assessments for both your intelligence (IQ) and emotional intelligence (EQ).

All of these assessments are very helpful in fine-tuning who you really are and discovering your Authenticity Advantage.

I have already described the importance of taking a personality assessment, as well as the invaluable information you can receive from taking the CliftonStrengths Assessment. But I have yet to mention the Seven Pillars of Thought, IQ, or EQ and how they can help you in your quest for authenticity.

Your Best Thinking

Since the early 1980s, Dr. Caroline Leaf has researched the mind-brain connection. She discovered there are seven basic types of thought and writes about them in her book *The Gift in You*. Each type of thought takes place in a different area in the brain.

She says everyone uses all seven types of thought, but they seem to take precedence in an order that depends on how you are wired. Discovering your dominant thought type can be very useful in determining how you do your best thinking. If you have a problem you need to think through, discovering where and how you think can help you in focusing on the best solutions. And, as usual, we don't all think the same way. One of these seven types of thinking will probably resonate with you.

1. Intrapersonal

If your dominant way of thinking is intrapersonal, then you will receive information best by reflection and introspection. You probably prefer a quiet place with no distractions when you really need to think.

Intrapersonal thinkers can control their thoughts and emotions, prefer to work independently, are curious about the meaning of life, and empower and encourage others.

2. Interpersonal

If your dominant way of thinking is interpersonal, then you will receive information best by communicating. You probably notice that your brain really begins to work when you start talking.

Interpersonal thinkers can understand and work well with people, they like social interaction and building relationships, they are good at mediating disputes, and they love to talk.

3. Linguistic

If your dominant way of thinking is linguistic, then words (spoken, written, expressed, or read) are how you primarily form thoughts. While others may think in terms of sounds or pictures, you think in words that have precise meaning.

Linguistic thinkers care about semantics, they like to argue and persuade, they have a good memory for names, dates, and places, and they ask a lot of questions.

4. Logical/Mathematical

If your dominant way of thinking is logical/mathematical, then reasoning is primarily how you form thoughts. As Spock from Star Trek might say, if it isn't logical it won't compute.

Logical/Mathematical thinkers can manipulate and use numbers effectively, they like to reason things out, they like to identify and find meanings in things, and they are intuitive and disciplined in their thinking.

5. Kinesthetic

If your dominant way of thinking is kinesthetic, then movement and touch are how you primarily form thoughts. If your mind is working on something, then your body is probably in motion.

Kinesthetic thinkers have good coordination, they enjoy exercise, they have a good sense of timing, and they need to move when thinking.

6. Musical

If your dominant way of thinking is musical, then you primarily build memory through rhythm and intuition. When you are pondering something, you probably can be found whistling, humming, or playing a rhythm with your hands or feet. You can do your best thinking while listening to music.

Musical thinkers can read people through tone of voice and body language, instinctively feel when things are right or wrong, interpret the meaning behind things, and respond to music.

7. *Visual/Spatial*

If your dominant way of thinking is visual/spatial, then you think through abstract language and imagery. If you are a builder or an artist, you can probably see the finished work before it is started.

Visual/Spatial thinkers navigate through spaces (traffic) well, recognize faces but may not remember names, think in pictures and visualize details, and may stare off into space when listening to someone.

The different types of thought remind me of people in my life who exemplify some of these thought patterns. A friend of mine from my Marine Corps days attended the same staff meetings that I had to attend every week. His thinking combined the linguistic and interpersonal styles. It was as if someone would push a button on him sometime during the staff meeting, and he would just start to talk. Ninety-five percent of what he said was seemingly unimportant, but the other 5 percent was brilliant.

After a while, most of the rest of us in the staff meetings learned that it was worth suffering through the 95 percent to get to the 5 percent. I can't help smiling at the thought of him talking and of how many times we had to tell him to shut up.

Dr. Leaf describes one of the CEOs she worked with who was a kinesthetic thinker. He had to be moving to function in his role at work. As you can imagine, this probably drove some of his co-workers nuts. Dr. Leaf's solution was to have him sit on a big rubber ball instead of a chair, and it worked. I might recommend that solution to a friend of mine who cannot stand still. If he is standing in any one place for more than a couple of seconds, he must start rocking from side to side, as if he is standing on the deck of a ship that is rolling with the waves. I get seasick just looking at him.

My dad was a visual/spatial thinker. He could see something in his mind that he was going to build before he started. He was also a gifted artist. Before he began a portrait, he could see the finished painting. His final career as a graphic artist fit his thinking style well.

A big portion of becoming an authentic person is recognizing how you think. The seven types of thought show that we do not all think the same way, but they can also help you discover the way you think best. If you are an intrapersonal thinker, you may need to find a quiet place with no distractions to do your best thinking. If you are an interpersonal thinker, you may need to start talking before the ideas begin to flow. Maybe your best thinking comes when you are moving or listening to music.

The point is that there is no cookie-cutter solution because we are all very different people. Find your best way to think and use it as much as possible. This is part of your Authenticity Advantage.

IQ and EQ

Intelligence Quotient (IQ) is a measure of a person's reasoning ability. It is an indicator of how well someone can use information and logic to answer questions or make predictions. In other words, it measures how well someone can learn.

IQ tests have been around for over 100 years and became popular in World War I as a way to assess men coming into the Army and their fitness for duty in battle. Since then, IQ tests have become a major factor in describing someone's intelligence. An IQ of 100 is considered normal, and most people score between 85 and 115. A score of 132 or higher will allow you into the Mensa club and 160 or higher is considered genius level.

Emotional Quotient (EQ) is something much different and is gaining popularity in the business world. *Emotional Intelligence*, a book by Travis Bradberry states:

Emotional Intelligence is your ability to recognize and understand emotions in yourself and others, and your ability to use this awareness to manage your behavior and relationships…It affects how we manage behavior, navigate social complexities, and make personal decisions to achieve positive results.

There is no known connection between IQ and EQ.

According to Bradberry, your IQ and your personality cannot be changed, but your EQ can. He points out that your EQ is the biggest predictor of your performance and excellence. His research has also found that people with higher EQs make more money.

EQ is made up of four components.

1. Self-Awareness
2. Self-Management
3. Social Awareness
4. Relationship Management

Of the four components, Self-Awareness is the biggest indicator of performance. Eighty-three percent of top performers have high Self-Awareness with no correlation to their IQ. From an Authenticity Advantage point of view, it is much more advantageous to have a high EQ than a high IQ.

The six aspects of who you are that have already been discussed are all ways of increasing your Self-Awareness. If you take this seriously it could move you into the ranks of the top performers.

If you have been blessed with a high IQ and you can learn to improve your EQ as well, then all the better. But if you weren't born exceptionally intelligent, then there is nothing holding you back. For some of us, that's a relief.

Accurate Thinking

Your GIFT is your very unique way of thinking, which shows up in a talent you can develop to greatness. That is what separates you from everybody else who has ever lived.

In the introduction to Napoleon Hill's famous book on success, *Think and Grow Rich*, he writes:

> *In every chapter of this book, mention is made of the money-making secret which has made fortunes for hundreds of exceedingly wealthy men whom I have carefully analyzed over a long period of years.*

The exceedingly wealthy men he refers to are Henry Ford, William Wrigley, Jr., John Wanamaker, George Eastman, Charles Schwab, Theodore Roosevelt, William Jennings Bryan, Thomas Edison, and many more. If these people knew a secret about making money, and it was revealed in a book, wouldn't you want to know what it is? And yet countless people have read *Think and Grow Rich* without discovering the secret. I'll give you a hint—the secret is on the cover!

The secret that the wealthy have discovered is how to think. You must *Think* to *Grow Rich*. But what does it mean to think? Doesn't everybody think? Apparently not. According to Thomas Edison:

> *Five percent of the people think; ten percent of the people think they think, and the other eighty-five percent would rather die than think.*

The more I dug into the idea that most people don't really think, I began to ask a logical question: Why don't they? Here is what some famous people had to say on that subject:

> *Thinking is the hardest work there is, which is probably the reason so few engage in it.* — *Henry Ford*

> *Simple can be harder than complex: You have to work hard to get your thinking clean to make it simple. But it's worth it in the end because once you get there, you can move mountains.* — *Steve Jobs*

> *People don't like to think. If one thinks, one must reach conclusions. Conclusions are not always pleasant.* — *Helen Keller*

> *I insist on a lot of time being spent, almost every day, to just sit and think. That is very uncommon in American business. I read and think. So, I do more reading and thinking and make fewer impulse decisions than most people in business. I do it because I like this kind of life.* — *Warren Buffett*

With those quotes in mind, what does it mean to think? You might say that is a silly question, but the reality is that most people use their feelings and emotions rather than thinking things through. Feelings and emotions are mental reactions or sensations based on perception or unreasoned opinion.

People who "think" with their emotions or feelings don't originate thoughts or use reason; they merely react to things. This kind of "thinking" can be emotionally exhausting but it doesn't take any effort. That is what is meant by having a low Emotional Intelligence (EQ) score. A low EQ represents a person whose thoughts never pass through the limbic system of their brain to reach the frontal lobe. They do not apply reason or logic to the information they receive.

Thought, on the other hand, is a developed intention or plan that engages reasoning power and the power to imagine or conceive. Thinking means that you reflect or ponder in your mind, that you form a mental picture or exercise the powers of judgment, conception, or reason. It requires imagination and effort.

> *First comes thought; then organization of that*
> *thought, into ideas and plans; then transformation of*
> *those plans into reality. The beginning, as you will*
> *observe, is in your imagination.* — *Napoleon Hill*

Napoleon Hill describes accurate thinking as a process. The first step in the process is to separate emotions and opinions from facts. Then facts are categorized into relevant and non-relevant facts, discarding the non-relevant facts to make accurate decisions. This is the basis of accurate thinking. To think accurately you need to have a high EQ; and, fortunately, this can be learned.

Hill takes the idea of accurate thought one step further. Beyond making decisions based on relevant facts is a level called creative thinking. This goes past the rearranging of known facts and concepts. Using creative imagination and prayer, new thoughts are created for the application of a purpose.

Creative thought is something we should all aspire to, but the sad fact is that most people never get past purely emotional thought. Now that you know that there is a difference and there is something you can do about it, applying accurate thought, and possibly creative thought, to your purpose will give you an even greater advantage in your authenticity.

Chapter 8
Lead or Follow?

A **major part of being authentic is knowing whether you**
are a leader or a follower. Especially if you are an American,
there is undue stress heaped on people to become leaders. If you are a
natural-born leader, no problem; but what if you aren't. On the other
hand, many natural leaders have been coached by parents, teachers, or
well-meaning friends to not be so bossy; and they have taken it to heart.
These leaders try to be followers to appease others. Knowing whether
you are naturally a leader or a follower makes a big difference.

There is an age-old debate over whether leaders are born or
made. Those who believe that leaders can be made will say that anyone can be trained to lead or that people rise to leadership based on
the situation. Those that believe that leaders are born will acknowledge that people can be in "leadership roles" without being natural
leaders, but real leaders are born that way. Part of this debate results
because we have elevated leadership to such a high level that being a
follower is considered inferior. Not so! Can you imagine if everyone
was a leader? It would be chaos.

We often confuse management and leadership. Managers manage assets, while leaders inspire people to follow. Many managers
consider employees to be assets, so we often put managers in charge
of people and call them leaders. If you have ever had to report to
a manager you know what I mean. If you have the good fortune to
work for a leader, while you may not have been able to put it into
words, you know he or she was a leader and not a manager.

Much has been written about leadership, and there are numerous leadership development courses. The problem that I see with

these courses is that no one defines what leadership is, so people walk away confused. If your "leader" is confused, what do you think happens to his team? See the problem?

The modern idea of what we call leadership is pretty new. The oldest concept of leadership had to do with going first, as in a leader going into battle in front of the troops. Before 1800, a person in a position of what we now call "leadership" was someone who had been delegated authority in certain matters. The one that delegated the authority was either the king or the ruler of that country.

Leaders may have been delegated authority, but there is a difference between authority and responsibility. The one who delegates the authority cannot delegate responsibility. Putting this another way, authority can be delegated, but responsibility cannot. A husband can delegate authority to his wife, but he is still responsible for the family. A president can delegate authority to his cabinet, but he is still responsible for the country. The CEO of a company can delegate authority to her executives, but she is still responsible for the company. A commanding officer can delegate to his captains, but he is still responsible for his command. A police or fire chief can delegate authority to commanders, but they are still responsible for what happens in a given situation. That is why leaders need to inspire their followers instead of managing them. As a leader, you cannot manage every action, but you can inspire your people to do the right thing.

Trying to exercise authority without the corresponding GIFT will result in catastrophe. If you are doing anything that does not correspond to your personality or your GIFT, it will take enormous effort and probably leave you frustrated and exhausted. We have already said that who you are and your GIFT were given to you at birth. You did nothing to earn them. That is how leadership is: it is part of who you are—naturally.

People whose personality is high in the D quadrant are natural leaders. They want to be in charge everywhere they go, in everything they do. They might be able to tone it down, but they can't turn it off. This is how my wife is. Even though we both have high D traits as part of our personalities, hers is higher. Mary naturally tells people what to do, and in a way that is not offending. Most of the time, the people she tells what to do end up doing exactly what she says and with smiles on their faces. She's in charge, and they know it. That is part of her GIFT. In many areas of our marriage, she is the leader. I laugh as I write this because maturing enough to recognize her natural leadership didn't come smoothly or easily. Even though I am ultimately responsible for our family, recognizing her GIFT of leadership has made a huge difference for us.

When someone without the GIFT of leadership tries to tell people what to do, the people either complain or just comply because they know he or she is the boss and they have to do as told if they want to keep their jobs. Many military and law enforcement "leaders" who transition to the "real world" realize their leadership skills ended when they took off their uniforms. The respect they had from their military or law enforcement subordinates was not because of any leadership abilities but because of the respect due to the rank they held. The point is that people who are natural leaders have the personality and GIFT to lead.

However, I have learned that there is an exception. There are some people without high D personality traits that exhibit situational leadership. Their leadership is usually confined to their area of expertise. In a case like this, the person might be an excellent leader at work but won't speak up at a PTA meeting or take a leadership role in a civic or church group. It would be a mistake to think that such a "situational leader" could lead in an area outside their area of expertise. A natural leader with high D personality traits will want to lead all the time.

This answers the question about whether leaders are born or if people can be trained to be leaders. Leaders lead. They can't help it. A natural leader will always be a better leader than one who tries to lead without the personality and corresponding GIFT for it. The authority for these natural leaders comes from the same source as their GIFT. But—and it's a big BUT—leadership can be abused if it doesn't have a purpose. Purpose-driven leadership is an excellent thing to behold. Followers naturally want to follow these kinds of leaders.

Who Is a Leader?

I define a leader as someone who possesses these four traits:

1. Leaders know who they are. They know their Identities and their GIFT.
2. Leaders know the GIFTs of others, especially those who work for them, and they place them in the best positions based on their GIFTs.
3. Leaders believe in and are able to communicate vision. A vision is the direction an organization is headed and the expected outcome of heading that way. It is a mental image of what the future will be like. The vision may not necessarily be their own vision. A leader without vision (their own or someone else's) is a manager. This is not derogatory.
4. Leaders inspire others to follow the vision. They give clear directions to followers and lead by example. They exhort and encourage followers to be their best.

> ### *A leader without vision is a manager.*

Who Is a Follower?

As you can tell, I don't believe everyone is a natural-born leader. Most of us are meant to be followers. It has been said, "A leader without followers is simply a man going for a walk." As I have already mentioned, a lot has been written about leadership. You can find books and articles written on leadership in business, in the military, in sports, in politics, and in the Church. Most of those writings deal with being in charge of a group of people that already exists and getting them to do something. How you get them to do what you want determines what kind of leader you are...or so the mainstream thinking goes.

What is really interesting is what followers say about leaders! *Strengths Based Leadership*, by Tom Rath and Barry Conchie published findings based on a 2005-2008 study conducted by Gallup, and these findings aren't guesswork or opinion. What they found out is not what "leaders" expected. Followers did *not* describe leaders with words like vision, purpose, charisma, wisdom, humor, or dynamic speaker. Those are the kinds of words that leaders used.

Instead, the words that followers chose to describe leaders they follow showed a distinct pattern. According to Rath and Conchie, "In some cases, more than 1000 people had listed exactly the same word, without any categories or options provided. Given that there are more than 170,000 words in the English language, this was impressive." Here are the top four:

1. Trust

The top word used to describe leaders they follow is *trust*. Closely related to trust were words like *honesty*, *integrity*, and *respect*. One of the things it takes for followers to trust a leader is time. The most common response was that they knew their leader for 10 years, and at least 75 percent of the followers said they knew their leader for six years or more. It takes time to know if a leader is trustworthy and has a proven track record.

Organizations that have trustworthy leaders seldom spoke about trust. On the other hand, organizations that had issues with honesty, integrity, and respect spoke about trust frequently. So, if you are evaluating a company to apply your GIFT to, and the leadership talks a lot about *trust, honesty, integrity,* and *respect,* it could be a red flag.

2. Compassion

The second word that came up was *compassion*. A leader who inspires others to follow makes you feel that you are cared for as a person. Followers of compassionate leaders are more likely to stay with an organization and less likely to job hop. They are more likely to engage their customers, be more productive, and be more profitable for the organization. Leaders who exhibit compassion use positive energy with their followers. They emphasize the good rather than the bad because people don't want to follow negative people around.

3. Stability

Followers used words like *security, strength, support,* and *peace* to describe the leaders they could always count on, so *stability* ranked high with them. The 2005-2008 study found that "as a leader, your followers also need to know that your core values are stable, and nothing creates stability as quickly as transparency." There is a double standard concerning leaders and followers: Followers think it may be all right for their truth to be "relative" and for them to live without absolutes; but when it comes to their leaders, people want to know that they tell the truth, and their truth cannot be relative.

Followers feel that a leader who operates in the gray area does not inspire confidence because they never really know where the leader stands. If your "leader" says that what he does on his own time is none of your business—beware! What's he hiding?

4. Hope

While followers want stability in their leaders for today, they also want leaders to give them *hope* for the future. Other words they expressed for the word hope were *direction, faith,* and *guidance.*

Followers want leaders to have a vision for the future and a path to get them there. The study found that when followers have hope they are 69 percent more engaged in the activities of the vision. When people do not have hope or are not enthusiastic about their future, they lose confidence, disengage from their work, and feel helpless.

When followers see a leader moving from one crisis to the next and constantly reacting to conditions, they sense the leader is out of control. If leaders are not cultivating and creating direction, faith, and guidance inside their organizations then no one else is either.

> *Hope deferred makes the heart sick, but desire fulfilled is a tree of life. —Proverb*

The point is that there are leaders and there are followers. Relatively few people are leaders, so that makes most people followers. One is not better than the other. If you don't know which you are, a leader or a follower, it will be very difficult to be authentic. A leader who tries to "fit in" ends up becoming frustrated and probably disruptive to the organization. A follower who is trying to be a leader will become equally frustrated, probably wondering why no one is following. This type of person will usually resort to using force rather than inspiration to keep subordinates in line.

When you recognize your place in an organization as either a leader or a follower, it gives you more confidence in using your GIFT. It will also allow others in the organization to use their GIFTs in a spirit of harmony. Leaders use their GIFTs to provide vision, direction, and inspiration. Followers use their GIFTs for everything else.

If you find yourself constantly having to prove yourself to others, you may be acting in the wrong role. Each person fits into a vision naturally, not by trying harder. If you feel like a square peg trying to fit in a round hole, part of the problem is that you may be a follower that is trying to lead or a leader that is trying not to rock the boat by attempting to fit in. Leaders lead...all the time. Followers follow.

Recognizing that you are really a follower may allow you to stop trying to be what you are not. It may free you to be the best you and to cultivate your GIFT to the fullest. The idea that everyone must climb the organizational ladder probably started with frustrated leaders. If you are happy being the expert in your field, that may be how you can make the greatest difference and find the greatest joy.

When you become the best follower you can be, as part of a vision you are excited about, it permits other followers to do the same. That's when comparison in an organization stops and harmony begins. That is when your GIFT combines with theirs instead of competing with them.

On the other hand, recognizing that you are a leader could help you to stop feeling guilty about not fitting in with the crowd. You don't need to be "buddies" with everyone. If, on the other hand, you do want to be buddies with everyone, that may be the clue you needed to discover that you aren't a leader.

A leader's priority is always the vision; that is part of your GIFT.

If you weren't focused on the vision, you know it would never happen. Knowing this, you realize that followers do not have that kind of focus...and they never will. That's your work—your purpose. Theirs is to develop their unique GIFTs, while yours is to cultivate harmony, communicate the vision, and direct their GIFTs. Both leaders and followers are necessary parts of the whole. That's their Authenticity Advantage.

Chapter 9
Hindrances

So far, I have talked about six aspects of who you are, how you think, and whether you are a leader or a follower. Taken together, these elements provide you with an excellent depiction of who you really are. However, I would be remiss if I didn't address the two biggest hindrances to your ever becoming truly authentic. The first is what can be called a "Father Fracture." The other is comparison. Both can stop you in your tracks if you let them.

Father Fracture

This is going to be a touchy subject. What follows is the number one reason that people don't know who they are. It is so emotionally and politically charged that I'll bet you won't hear this anywhere else. I just ask that as you read through it, you don't shoot the messenger.

I once heard a pastor from a large suburban Chicago church talk about something called a "Father Fracture." A Father Fracture is when you have (or had) a bad relationship (or no relationship) with your father. This will probably lead to having a difficult time having a good relationship (or any relationship, for that matter) with your Father (God).

A Father Fracture can occur when your father doesn't (or didn't) live up to his responsibilities. He may have been in the home, but he wasn't there for you. Maybe you never knew your father because he either died when you were young or he might have deserted your family. Maybe you had an abusive father. No matter the situation, if it wasn't positive, how does it make you feel when someone talks about a "father"? Probably not too good.

A Father Fracture is important to recognize because you get your identity from your father. When I say that to an audience, it is like dropping a bomb. That's exactly what I thought the first time I heard it. I think most of us instinctively know how much our identity is influenced by our fathers; but if you had a bad or absent dad, it is kind of hard to swallow.

When I say that you get your identity from your father, I am not speaking about your genetics. I am not talking about your appearance or any physical characteristics. I am speaking about the confidence and trust, or lack thereof, you get from your father. If he provides unconditional love and approves of you just for who you are, your sense of identity will be radically different from those who did not get that support from their fathers. Even if your mother loved and approved of you, it will not have the same effect as when you receive love and approval from your father. Many of those who have not received what they need from their fathers have no idea they are missing something vital.

I was teaching the idea of finding your purpose to a group of law enforcement leaders a while ago, and all was going well…until I got to the subject of the Father Fracture. The room grew quiet. Faces changed. Some looked inquisitive, like I sparked their interest. Others withdrew.

After the training, several of the seasoned cops came up to me privately. They each mentioned that they thought what I said was true, even if it picked a few scabs. What they wanted to know was if I could prove it. Was there evidence that the Father Fracture was real and that one's identity comes from the father? They were interested for themselves, but they intuitively understood how this idea affected the populations they dealt with daily. Well, it turns out there is plenty of evidence, and it is a huge problem that is only getting worse. The challenge is that no one wants to touch this problem with a ten-foot pole.

David Blankenhorn wrote *Fatherless America* in 1995. His research and references on the subject are very thorough. Since the book was published, the problems he described have only gotten worse. So, for those of you who like to see the facts, here are some of the issues and statistics found by Blankenhorn (I have updated the numbers based on the most recent sources available.)

One of the factors I found remarkable is that until the mid-1800s it was the father, not the mother, who had the primary responsibility for child training, religious and moral education, and societal guidance. It was industrialization that caused the change. Once fathers had to go to work in a factory and be away from the family all day, these roles shifted to mothers.

Fatherlessness is the leading cause of poverty in America. In 2014, 23.6% of children lived in father-absent homes, according to the US Census Bureau. Fifty percent of all children will live in a single-parent home at some time before they reach age 18. In 2012, 41% of US children were born to never-married parents, according to the National Center for Health Statistics. Blankenhorn says that half of all children living with a single mother are in poverty, which is five times higher than children living with both parents.

The effects of fatherlessness can be devastating. For instance, child abuse is more likely to occur in single-parent homes than when both parents are present. There is also a greater risk of drug abuse, alcohol abuse, mental illness, suicide, and poor educational performance in single-parent homes. In women, there is an increase in promiscuity and teenage pregnancy; and in men, there is increased violence and criminality.

Involved fathers seem to have a special influence on the development of empathy in children. They stress ideas like competition, challenge, initiative, risk-taking, and independence. Mothers, on the other hand, are the caretakers. They stress personal safety and emotional security.

I think you can see that both mothers and fathers are necessary for the development of children. To diminish the role of either fathers or mothers would be a mistake, one that we seem to be making these days. If you didn't receive the unconditional love that your father was supposed to give you, you would have no example by which to fully recognize the unconditional love your Father (God) has for you. Unfortunately, that describes more and more children and young adults.

Many people I speak with today grew up in single-parent families and consider their single-parent families as "normal." Other people say they were fortunate to have their father in the home when they grew up, even though their dad was rarely ever there. If that describes your dad, did he help you, guide you, and provide leadership in your family? Or did your mom do those things? The point is that even families with two parents often have a dad who is absent from the children. Does any of this relate to you?

A friend and I were talking about personalities one day when I brought up the subject of his father. When I asked him how often his father told him he loved him or that he was proud of him, my friend said "never." He said he didn't have "that kind of a relationship" with his father. That statement baffled me. What kind of relationship did he think he was supposed to have?

The more I checked into this question, the more I realized most men and women don't know what a proper relationship with their father is supposed to look like. That is because they have never seen one.

> *Most people don't know what a proper relationship with their father is supposed to look like.*

My Dad as an Example

I asked my wife about this and was surprised by her answer. Her dad died when she was a teenager. Before his passing, he and Mary's mother were separated. There was major tension in their home and a lot of stress and alcohol abuse. So, when I asked Mary what she thought a good relationship with a father should look like, she told me she saw it in my father. She told me how awesome it was for her to see my mother sitting on my father's lap the first time she came over to our home. Having grown up in a home with a strong and loving father, I took it for granted. My late dad was by no means perfect, but he is still the best example I know for what a father is supposed to be.

The interesting thing about my dad is that he had a huge Father Fracture of his own. As a teenager, he left home after his tenth-grade year and joined the Marine Corps. The year was 1939, and since the US had not yet entered World War II, he didn't join the Marines out of patriotic fervor. He just wanted to get out of his home situation. His father had not gotten along too well with his mother, and his father had a bad habit of spending his paycheck on drinking and "playing the ponies." As the middle of six kids in a rough neighborhood in Philadelphia, my father needed to escape.

By the time I came along, Dad had fought in World War II and Korea. He was the picture of the perfect Marine first sergeant; he had a booming command voice and all the medals to go with it. If he looked into your eyes, you would swear he could see right into your soul. It was impossible to lie to him.

This same tough, rugged, highly respected man tucked my sister and me into bed every night. Before we were tucked in, my mom, my sister, my dad, and I would all kneel by our beds to say prayers. Every night Dad would ask me if I was warm enough, and then he'd kiss me before he left the room. I never once had to guess if my parents loved me.

As I grew, Dad was always there for me. I remember, as a teenager, agreeing to take another guy's Sunday morning paper route for him while he went on vacation. At 4 a.m. on a Sunday morning, I waited on a corner a block away from our house for newspapers to be dropped off. It was dark, I had no flashlight, and rain began to fall. I had no idea what I was doing. I walked home with the papers and sat in the kitchen, crying as I started to wrap the newspapers in plastic.

I didn't want to wake Dad up because I wanted him to be proud of me, not see me looking like a basket case. Dad must have heard me because he dressed and came downstairs. He never complained about the time or told me how stupid I was; he just helped me deliver the papers. When we were done, he put his arm around me and then went back to bed. Needless to say, I didn't last as a paperboy.

My friend did not have those kinds of experiences with his father; neither did my wife. Only after hearing the pastor in Chicago speak about the Father Fracture did I realize how truly blessed I was to have grown up with a real father. No matter what I did, or did not do, my father always told me how proud he was of me and that he loved me. He gave me my identity as an approved son of a great man.

I fully realize that some of you who are reading this had a father as good as mine, or better. But most of you did not. Realizing that you have a Father Fracture is 90% of the battle. Until you deal with it, you will not have a firm foundation from which to move forward.

When you have had the approval of your father, without having had to earn it, you have a source of confidence that lasts a lifetime. When you *know* you are loved by your father, no matter what you do or don't do, the natural result is to want to please him. You won't need anyone else's approval to make you feel complete.

Having your dad tell you he is proud of you, and knowing that his pride is not coming from your performance, instills a sense of confidence in you that no one can remove. For whatever reason, this support is more important and has a greater effect on you when it comes from your father rather than from your mother. Somehow, mothers are expected to have these feelings and express them to their children, and it is vitally important to us to have them from our mothers. But if children don't get them from their fathers, very important pieces of their identities will be missing.

Ultimately, a good father has one crucial task. By being a good father—one who loves, approves, protects, provides for, teaches, and guides his children—he teaches his children about the nature of God. Unfortunately, many fathers in today's society have not done a very good job.

For much of society, the word *father* does not conjure up any of the attributes it should; instead, it is often viewed as a bad word, leaving people feeling neglected, abandoned, or abused. It is no wonder that people are leaving mainline denominations. Who would want to belong to a religion that calls God the Father when they have no idea how good He really is?

Healing a Father Fracture has two parts. First, recognize you have one. You can't fix what you don't know, or won't admit, is broken. If your father did not give you unconditional love, made you work for it, or wasn't there for you, that's not your fault. He did not fulfill his role in helping you form your identity.

Second, find out for yourself (yes, it is up to you, and no one else can do this for you) that your Father (God) really does love you, approves of you, protects you, provides for you, teaches you, and guides you. He's the one who gave you your personality, your GIFT, and your purpose. He chose these qualities specifically for you because He wants more for you than you want for yourself. Even if your father blew it, your Father doesn't.

I believe this issue called Father Fracture is a huge problem that is only getting worse. Until you deal with this issue, and everyone has a Father Fracture to some degree, it will be very difficult for you to find your authentic self.

Comparison

The other major hindrance to becoming an authentic person is comparison. When you compare, you are examining the character or qualities of someone else. When you compare yourself to others, you are trying to figure out if you have more value than they do… or if they have more value than you. Both are wrong, and both are dangerous.

Comparison can be very insidious and often slides into our lives without us even realizing it. When Mary and I were first married we bought a new house in a new development. Even though most of the people in the neighborhood moved in around the same time, we were the last couple on the block to put in a yard. Others had lush green grass and plants in their front yards while we had dirt.

To be honest, we barely qualified for the house we bought and were glad to just be living there. This was where comparison set in. We imagined that everyone else must be making more money and doing much better financially than we were, even though it didn't seem that way. How could they afford to have such nice yards?

One night, our neighbors across the street, who had the same house model as us, went out somewhere. So, I snuck across the street to peek inside their living room window. I was shocked! They had no living room furniture...but they had a nice yard. At least we had furniture. Our assumptions about our neighbors had been all wrong. Trying to keep up with your friends and neighbors leads to comparison; but things are rarely what they seem.

As you figure out who you are, you might compare your personality to someone else's. You might think that people in leadership positions or those you consider to be more popular have better personalities than you. They don't have better personalities; they are just different. And if you are more popular than them, you aren't better, you are just different. Your personality is perfect for you.

As you discover your GIFT, it might be easy to compare your GIFT to a GIFT you admire in someone else. Again, you can easily fall into the trap of thinking that another's GIFT is better than yours. When you realize that your GIFT is the unique way that you are wired to think, you can see that one GIFT is not better than another; they are just different.

The real, and potentially most damaging, comparison comes when we compare what we do with our GIFT to what others do with theirs. You probably don't know other people's purposes or if they have achieved them. We all like to hear about the fame that can come from people using their GIFTs, but what does that have to do with you? This kind of comparison can keep you from making a difference. If you focus on being the best you, the rewards that come will be perfect for you.

> ## Comparison is the thief of joy.
> ## —Theodore Roosevelt

Whenever people compare who they are, their GIFTs, their desires, or their visions to those of others, they are setting themselves up for disaster. If you happen to fall victim to the trap of comparison, it will probably be because you have compared your greatest weakness to someone else's greatest strength. There are two major problems with that.

First, your purpose can only be achieved when you act from your strengths, not your weaknesses. You know your weaknesses better than anyone else. It is absolutely fine to admire people who are strong where you are weak. In fact, it is essential that you recognize those people. None of us can accomplish a vision by ourselves, and a good leader will find people who have strengths in different areas.

Before you compare yourself to someone else, remember your strengths. Your greatest strength (your GIFT) is probably in an area where the person you are comparing yourself to is weak. Rather than being jealous of each other, you will find that working together will create greater results.

Second, we tend to assume people are strong in the areas we observe. When you take the time to get to know people, you will often find that they are pretending to be good in the areas you are jealous of. They put up a façade to impress others, but privately what you are jealous of is exhausting and unfulfilling to them. They became trapped by the masks they chose to wear and wish they could find their true GIFTs. They are probably envious of you. So, what are you jealous of?

Social media has exacerbated this issue. People rarely tell you how much they struggle on their posts. In fact, most will go out of their way to only show you how cool, beautiful, and all-together they are. The funny thing is that studies have shown that many selfies and Instagram posts have been altered to give you a false impression. If you want to be authentic and associate with other authentic people, skip social media and go see them in person.

The bottom line is that the only comparison you should be engaged in is comparing where you are now to where you want to be. If you are on track with your purpose, then great, keep up the good work. If you are not where you want to be, then self-correct or get with your mentor to find a good course of action.

Your authenticity is too important to become sidetracked by comparison. You have the right personality, the right GIFT, and the right desire to fulfill all you were created to be. When you become the best you, and you know it, you won't be tempted to compare yourself to anyone. That is how you make a difference.

Chapter 10
Applying Your Authenticity Advantage

Confidence

Ultimately, becoming your best, authentic self results in you having more confidence. Confidence enables you to take the risks you need to be successful, and it enables you to try things outside your comfort zone.

I tried parachuting, scuba diving, and flying, all of which were outside my comfort zone. I tried out for major league baseball, played rugby in the Marine Corps, and ran two marathons. Those were definitely out of my comfort zone. I tried working a job, then a career, and I worked as an entrepreneur. I worked for a paycheck, for a bonus, for all commission, and then I worked for myself. Without confidence in who I am, I would still be working a job in someone else's company and accepting whatever came my way.

I am not saying that you need to do what I did, but trying different paths is part of discovering what works best for you; and confidence in yourself allows you to find your best path.

The six aspects of who you really are (your personality, your gender, your generation, how you think about money, how you give and receive love, and your GIFT) will combine to give you the most complete picture of your authentic self. Without understanding those six aspects, it will be difficult to think accurately. That is why so many people drift through life instead of living with purpose.

Understanding yourself gives you an advantage in finding the right career and in establishing lasting relationships. Your Authenticity Advantage will help you to eliminate all the careers you should not engage in and to focus on those that naturally fit who you are. Discoveries, like knowing if you are a leader or follower, can make a huge difference in the decisions you make in your career and in your relationships. It not only determines your actions but also how others perceive and respond to you.

Accurate thinking plays a large role in developing lasting relationships. While most people build relationships entirely on emotion, those who think accurately build relationships on purpose. The relationships you form, whether personal or professional, will be based on the real you without ulterior motives.

You will find that when you are genuine with other people they usually reciprocate. This makes for relationships based on the truth. When you are sincere with other people, those who are not in agreement with your purpose will tell you. Knowing where you stand with other people makes finding the right partners much easier.

Trust

Whether you are a leader or a follower, we all have trust issues. A major part of those issues is a lack of authenticity. People find it increasingly difficult to trust politicians, the media, our employers, and even the Church. And our lack of trust in personal relationships is at an all-time high. Why is that?

Part of the reason is that so few people know who they are. They portray an image of themselves that is less than authentic. Some of us have been fooled by an inauthentic person once too often, and now we find it safer to not trust others…at least until they can prove themselves. Building trust takes time, but destroying trust can happen in an instant.

Whenever you meet people, you make both conscious and subconscious decisions about them within seconds. You either decide you like them enough to allow a relationship (professional or personal) to continue to develop, or you don't like them. You could also decide that you can't get a read on them or that something seems off about them. Being authentic allows people to get an accurate read on you so they can decide if they like you or not. It also allows you to get an accurate read on others. This is the foundation of trust.

Creating an atmosphere of trust is critical in any profession. A leader who is authentic will inspire the people he is leading rather than having to force them to do things. Employees who trust their management are much more likely to be engaged in their work. The result is more productivity, less employee turnover, and a more fun work environment. A salesperson who is faking who they are just to get a sale usually turns people off, but a salesperson who authentically wants the best for a customer may have found a customer for life. Whenever people can't tell where you are coming from because you are not authentic, trust breaks down and the environment becomes toxic.

Our personal relationships are also influenced by the trust that comes from being authentic. We have all had occasions where we have said things like, "I can't get a read on that guy" or "What do they want from me?" In those cases, others may be hiding their true selves from you in order to manipulate you or to create an advantage for some reason. How much trust does that generate? How strong will that relationship be, and how long will it last?

Creating a sense of trust is a vital part of all human relationships. Whether you are a leader, a professional, an employee, a salesperson, or someone who is searching for a lasting personal relationship, being your authentic self will help to foster trust in others. Being authentic will also enable you to detect others who are authentic with you. Real communication and trust come from both parties being authentic.

What Do You Want to Do?

Once you know who you really are and your GIFT, determining what you want to do becomes much easier.

> ### You have to BE before you can DO and DO before you can HAVE. —Zig Ziglar

What you do should be the result of being who you are. But most people don't follow this path. They start doing without paying attention to who they are, and then they wonder why they feel that something is missing.

When discussing the question of what you want to do, most people instantly reply with what they want to do for a job, career, or vocation. Their paths go something like this: they are told to go to school and get good grades so they can go to the right college so they can get into a good career field and work from 22 years old until they reach age 65 and then retire, hopefully with a large enough nest egg to carry them until they die.

They wish for careers they will like. They hope they will find some kind of purpose in what they do and will make some kind of difference. However, purpose and making a difference are secondary thoughts to making enough money to get by on. Consequently, few ever find their purpose or make a difference, and fulfillment is something for the lucky few...at least in a career. Does this sound familiar?

Some stay in a profession for which they have no passion because it pays well, and they are afraid to try something new. The term for that is wearing "Golden Handcuffs." Others will stay in a profession even if it doesn't pay well, only because that is all they know. They, too, are afraid to try something new, even if it could be something that they would be passionate about. Both are examples of a lack of confidence...confidence that comes with your Authenticity Advantage.

So, what's the key to doing what you want to do?

One of the greatest advantages of being authentic is discovering your GIFT. You will have a natural desire to use your GIFT, and employing it is your purpose. So, putting it another way, what you want to do is your purpose. The key is finding your GIFT. Employing your GIFT is the most authentic thing you can do with your life, and you'll never stop wanting to do it.

How you choose to use your GIFT is up to you and depends on who you are. You might want to use your GIFT in a career, or you might want to use it in an avocation.

If you want to use your GIFT in a career, it could be because of how you think about money. Your GIFT could generate the income you need to make a difference, like for a charity or foundation, or the income could be incidental compared to the fulfillment you find in your career.

If you want to use your GIFT in an avocation (a passion for which you are not paid) you may have a job that works for you, but you are more passionate about what you do outside of work. I have a friend who had a career as a surgeon, but his avocation is volunteering with Doctors Without Borders. Even though he has retired from his paid profession, he still uses his GIFT as an avocation. That is the mark of a GIFT; it is something from which you never retire.

What you actually want to do, whether you realize it or not, is to employ your GIFT. That is why you were created. You will have a natural desire to use your GIFT, and the passion to apply it to something you feel emotional about comes with the GIFT.

What Do You Want to Have?

If what you think you want to have is the result of an advertisement on TV, the radio, the internet, social media, or because your friends all have it, you will soon become disappointed. The desires of your heart do not come from external influences. What you really want to have comes from your heart, from the inside. Those are the things that bring satisfaction and fulfillment.

Please do not hear what I am *not* saying. Wanting to have things is not bad; it is entirely natural. What I am saying is that what you want to have is the result of what you do, which in turn is the result of who you are. The things you want to have are because they help you to fulfill your purpose and because they are the result of what you do. So, if you must go into debt to get things you think you want, it is much more likely the result of some slick marketing rather than some desire of your heart.

Whether you want more money, better relationships, a house, a car, a family, a spouse, a vacation, to give to a charity, or to create a legacy, these desires should be the result of your Authenticity Advantage. The uniqueness of who you are and what you do will fulfill the desires of your heart. That is the way God intended it.

If you find yourself chasing things by trying to be more competitive or modifying your behavior, then the things you chase will not bring you the happiness you seek. The adage I referenced in Chapter 5, "He whoever dies with the most stuff wins," is not true. People who say they have never known the desires of their heart have not found their Authenticity Advantage, but you will.

Advantages of Being Authentic

Because we are social beings, we all have a need to fit in. The problem is that the need to fit in also produces pressure for us to conform, to be like everyone else. Those who don't conform become excluded from the group. How does that make you feel? Anxious? Depressed? Wondering what's wrong?

So, we learn to conform to the world around us by adapting from who we really are to what is expected. We pretend to be what we are not, and it is exhausting!

There is no advantage in being the same as everyone else. If you want different results, then something has to change. When you decide to quit pretending to be something you are not, you'll discover there is an advantage to being your real, authentic self.

You may be:

◊ ready for a change
◊ looking for the right career
◊ part of a sales team
◊ part of a leadership team

Whatever your situation, you need to stop faking and start being authentic.

The advantage of becoming an authentic person is that you'll find:

1. It takes a lot less effort.

Faking always takes more effort than being authentic. Just remembering all the lies we tell ourselves and others, and then having to justify them, can be exhausting.

2. It is a lot more fun.

Being authentic allows you to let your guard down and not worry about what other people think about you. Being yourself with people you trust is fun.

3. You can make a lot more money.

Eight-three percent of top performers have high self-awareness, which is another way of saying they know who they are and what they want—they are authentic. Those top performers make an average of $29,000 more a year than low performers with low self-awareness. It pays to be authentic.

4. You will have much better relationships.

Anyone who has been in a relationship where the other person was not who you thought he or she was knows what a nightmare that can be. Great relationships are built on trust and good communication, both of which stem from being authentic. This is true for personal relationships as well as professional relationships.

Chapter 11

Ambush

You may find that just about the time you start to figure out who you really are and what you want, something comes along to knock you off track and make you feel like giving up. I call this being ambushed, and you need to watch out for potential ambush sites.

Several years ago, I was stationed at Camp Pendleton, California, where there was a story circulating about an infamous ambush on the base. It seems a platoon of Marines was practicing night ambushes on a warm southern California night. They had set up machine guns with blank ammunition at both ends of a path that they chose as the ambush site. They also set popup flares and explosive noise-making devices to simulate Claymore mines. The idea was to practice a night ambush on other Marines that were dressed up as bad guys. The "bad guys" were supposed to walk down the path at a predetermined time during the night and trigger the ambush.

As some of you may know, Southern California has some issues with immigrants crossing the border illegally from Mexico. It just so happens that one of the US Customs and Border Patrol checkpoints is on Interstate 5 along the coastline where it cuts through Camp Pendleton. Sometimes the immigrants get out of vehicles somewhere south of the checkpoint, walk through Camp Pendleton, and then meet back up with the vehicles and drivers somewhere north of the checkpoint.

As the night grew darker and the coastal fog started to roll in, one of the Marines in the ambushing platoon heard some movement. The platoon was quietly alerted that the "bad guys" were approaching their "kill zone." (A kill zone is where the ambushers have carefully planned their fire so that as many bad guys get killed as possible.) As the "bad guys" entered the kill zone, one of them tripped the popup flare. As soon as that happened, both machine guns started firing and the simulated Claymore mines were detonated. Then, all the Marines in the ambush platoon started firing rifles loaded with blanks. The sound and light from the weapons firing were spectacular.

Unfortunately, the "bad guys" in the kill zone weren't the Marines who were dressed as bad guys. Apparently, a group of immigrants had wandered into the area where the Marines were practicing. They inadvertently walked into the ambush site and triggered a life-altering event. After making it across the border, and about 50 miles inside the US, they probably thought they were almost home free…only to be ambushed by Marines at night! Can you imagine the shock they must have felt?

When I was a new Marine lieutenant at the Basic School in Quantico, Virginia, I was taught how to ambush bad guys, as well as what to do if ambushed. If you are ambushed, you can bet your enemy has chosen very carefully where he will spring the ambush. He plans to keep you in the kill zone, for as long as possible to inflict the most damage on you. The longer you stay in that zone, the less likely it is that you will get out alive. If you must think about what you are going to do after you are ambushed, there is a great likelihood you aren't going to make it.

That is why we practiced Immediate Action Drills. "Immediate Actions" are what you do, without having to think, if you get ambushed. Even though lying down to take cover is the most natural thing to do, we were taught to face the fire and attack through it. Now, if you have to think about it, you are never going to do that in a real ambush. But, if you practice it over and over until it becomes a habit, you just might actually walk into the line of fire instead of lying down to take cover. I don't know what they teach for Immediate Action Drills now, but whatever they teach, these drills can save your life in a combat situation.

The same holds for you. When you discover who you are and what you want, don't be surprised if you get ambushed. Your ambush could come in the form of your job being cut. It could come from someone jealous of your newfound confidence. It could come in the form of "Who do you think you are?" comments from people you love and trust. It could come from evaluating what you thought were truths, only to find out that they were assumptions...and they were wrong. In any case, if you get ambushed, you will need to know your Immediate Action Drills.

You can't afford to make up these Immediate Actions while you are in the middle of an ambush. You need to practice them until they become habitual. That way, when someone, or something, comes against you, you will know what to do.

Here are some suggestions for your Immediate Action Drills:

1. Get out of the ambush. If it is a person that is ambushing you, get away from them as quickly and politely as possible, even if it is a friend or family member. Do not argue with that person. As it says in How to Win Friends and Influence People by Dale Carnegie, "The only way to get the best of an argument is to avoid it."

2. Write out your "I Am" statement mentioned earlier and keep copies of it with you wherever you go. Repeat it out loud to yourself several times a day until it becomes a habit.

3. If you have a mentor, call him as soon as you are ambushed. You can't call them every time you feel sorry for

yourself; but when you are ambushed, your mentor can help you get up and out of the "kill zone." There is a caveat here; you must determine before the ambush that you will do what the mentor says. During an ambush is not the time to think about it.

Your Authenticity Advantage is too important for you to allow someone to steal it from you. You need to protect it and constantly develop it. Knowing what you will do in advance of an attack on your authenticity could be what enables you to succeed in the face of adversity.

Conclusion

The six aspects of who you really are fit together to give you a complete picture of who you are and how you think—your Authenticity Advantage. You will naturally desire to use your GIFT (the unique and special way you think as evidenced by a single talent that can be developed to greatness). Employing your GIFT is your purpose. That is what you were created to do.

So, what do you want to have? Once you find your GIFT, you will want to have all that your purpose enables you to have. Your Authenticity Advantage is the key to what you want.

The world doesn't want another pretender, we want the authentic you.

Resources

DISC Personality Assessment

"Discover Yourself" is an online personality test (assessment) for adults that generates a six-page personality report. This version is a popular, cost-effective assessment. Your personality report is customized based on your online assessment that will take you only about 15 to 20 minutes to complete. Concise, yet very helpful insights. Includes charts and your scores. Some may think of this as a "personality test" or a "personality quiz." This is not really a test—you cannot fail. There are no right or wrong answers, just your individual preferences. Please note that, even though this is a "mini" version of the report, the online assessment is the same one that we use for the full report.

This Discovery Report version includes the following:

◊ DISC Overview
◊ Summary description
◊ Words that describe you
◊ Strengths
◊ How to be your best
◊ Environment & Team Dynamics
◊ Personality Graphs

The DISC Personality Assessment can be found at:

*https://www.personality-insights.com/shop/
adult-disc-personality-
profile-concise-mini-version-6-
pages-english-discovery-report*

Top 5 CliftonStrengths

Top 5 CliftonStrengths Access is the ideal solution for people who want a quick, introductory approach to strengths-based development. It introduces you to the first 5 of your 34 CliftonStrengths themes and provides ideas for how to use your CliftonStrengths to succeed.

This digital product includes one access code to complete the CliftonStrengths assessment. Upon completion, you will receive personalized CliftonStrengths assessment results and supporting tools and resources, including a digital copy of the bestselling book *StrengthsFinder 2.0*.

You'll Get:

◊ Your Signature Themes Report—This report presents your top five so you can identify your dominant talents and start leading a strengths-based life.

◊ Strengths Insight Report—This guide offers an in-depth analysis of your top five. Unique to your specific combination of strengths, this report describes who you are in astonishing detail and provides you with a comprehensive understanding of yourself, your strengths and what makes you stand out.

◊ Strengths Insight and Action-Planning Guide—This guide provides an in-depth analysis of each of your top five, personalized based on your unique strengths profile. It also includes 10 action items for each to help you think about how to start building and applying your strengths every day.

CliftonStrengths assessments can be found at:

https://www. gallupstrengthscenter. com/product/en-us/10108/ top-5-cliftonstrengths- access?category=featured- products

The Five Love Languages

The 5 Love Languages® profile will give you a thorough analysis of your emotional communication preference. It will single out your primary love language, what it means, and how you can use it to connect with your loved one with intimacy and fulfillment.

The assessment consists of 30 paired statements where you select the statement that best defines what is most meaningful to you in your relationship as a couple. Allow 10 to 15 minutes to complete the profile. Take it when you are relaxed, and try not to rush through it.

The Five Love Languages Assessment can be found at:

http://www.5lovelanguages. com/profile

Endnotes

1. https://www.psychologytoday.com/us/blog/i-hear-you/201907/why-are-millennials-so-anxious-and-unhappy

2. https://www.forbes.com/sites/travisbradberry/2016/05/10/12-habits-of-genuine-people/?sh=781d6834461d

3. https://www.psychologytoday.com/us/blog/click-here-happiness/201904/develop-authenticity-20-ways-be-more-authentic-person

4. https://www.psychologytoday.com/us/blog/the-science-success/201208/you-are-probably-wrong-about-you

5. https://www.psychologytoday.com/us/blog/hope-relationships/201402/brain-differences-between-genders

Recommended Reading

As a Man Thinketh, James Allen

Before You Quit Your Job, Robert Kiyosaki

Cash Flow Quadrant, Robert Kiyosaki

Deadly Emotions, Dr. Don Colbert

Emotional Intelligence 2.0, Drs. Travis Bradberry and Jean Greaves

Employ Your GIFT, TJ Gilroy

Father Fracture, TJ Gilroy

Fatherless America, David Blankenhorn

Getting to Know You, Chris Carey

Good to Great, Jim Collins

Grown Up Digital, Don Tapscott

In Pursuit of Purpose, Myles Munroe

Master Key to Riches, Napoleon Hill

Personality Tree, Florence Littauer

Rich Dad Poor Dad, Robert Kiyosaki

Strengths Based Leadership, Tom Rath and Barry Conchie

StrengthsFinder 2.0, Tom Rath

Stress Less, Dr. Don Colbert

Succeed and Grow Rich Through Persuasion, Napoleon Hill

The 5 Love Languages, Gary Chapman

The GIFT in You, Dr. Caroline Leaf

The Holy Bible, God

The Millionaire Next Door, Thomas Stanley and William Danko

The New Retirementality, Mitch Anthony

The Power of Focus, Jack Canfield, Mark Victor Hansen and Les Hewitt

The Purpose Master Key, TJ Gilroy

Think and Grow Rich, Napoleon Hill

What Americans Really Want…Really, Dr. Frank Luntz

Who Do You Think You Are Anyway?, Robert Rohm

About the Author

Thomas J. Gilroy is an author, lecturer, and business-man. He and his wife Mary reside in Foxfire Village, NC. He grew up in Dale City, VA, and attended the University of Virginia before being commissioned as a Marine Officer. His military specialty was as an attack helicopter pilot, where he received the nickname "TJ."

TJ entered the business world after his Marine Corps career, eventually becoming an executive in the tactical equipment industry. He and Mary now own AuthenticityAdvantage.com, working with people to help them to find their Authenticity Advantage.

Early in his business career, TJ found that asking better questions resulted in receiving better answers.

Whether asking questions of his parents, his commanding officers in the Marine Corps, his wife Mary, his mentor Jack, his business associates, friends, or, most importantly, the Holy Spirit, the same always held true: ask good questions, get good answers. He also found that the times of his life where he was just drifting or was frustrated were also the times when he stopped asking questions.

Subsequently, the answers he found and put into practice are now available to you. His ardent hope for you is that you find your purpose and that you make the difference God intended.

Other Books by TJ Gilroy

Almost everyone has a **Father Fracture** to some degree. It affects our image, our ability to discover our GIFT and purpose, and it is the major reason why so few people ever make the difference for which they were created. Father Fracture represents an Identity Crisis of unprecedented scale.

In **Father Fracture** you will learn:

◊ What a Father Fracture is
◊ Indicators that you may have a Father Fracture
◊ Causes of a Father Fracture
◊ The effects of a Father Fracture
◊ And what you can do about it

In **Employ Your GIFT,** you will discover that:

◊ You have a Special GIFT – everyone does.
◊ It is special because only you have your GIFT.
◊ Employing your GIFT is your purpose.
◊ Operating in your GIFT is what makes a difference.

You can choose to continue to struggle, or you can choose to use your GIFT. Many books claim to be life-changing. **Employ Your GIFT** really is!

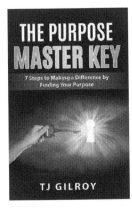

Are you wandering through life with no idea of why you were created? Are you even looking for an answer?

Is the whole idea of purpose too overwhelming?

Well, you are not alone.

The key to finding your purpose is to discover your special and unique GIFT because...your Purpose is to Employ Your GIFT.

But how do you discover your GIFT?

That's why TJ Gilroy wrote this "how-to" book. He shares the 7 key steps you can take to discover your GIFT so you can find your Purpose and make the difference for which you were created.

VISIT
www.TJGilroy.com